Praise for *All Pride, No Ego*

"Reading Jim's book is like talking with a friend or working with him every day on a project. We are honored to be included in his story and are inspired by his authentic leadership style and success."

SOFIA VERGARA and LUIS BALAGUER,
Actors, Producers, Entrepreneurs, and
Founders Latin World Entertainment

"Jim's personal and professional history offers a model to successfully navigate life's journey."

ANDY MOONEY,
CEO Fender

"If you're searching, eager to learn, and hungry for ways to make the world a better place, read Jim's book! In writing this amazing compendium of lessons drawn from his life and his career, Jim Fielding has shown us what it means to be open, curious, and vulnerable—all prerequisites for a life filled with meaning and impact. His journey is as unique as he is, but the lessons and how he navigated its challenges and joys are universal. We should all follow Jim's example and strive for the examined life, and then share it with others as Jim has done."

LAURIE BURNS MCROBBIE,
First Lady Emerita, Indiana University and
Founder, Women's Philanthropic Leadership Council

"Jim Fielding's *All Pride, No Ego* is inspiring, honest, funny, and candid. I learned about Jim, but I also took away lessons to apply to my own life—both personal and professional. And it is so *wonderfully* Midwestern. I know that it will have impact."

ANNE CAREY,
President Archer Gray Productions

"I consider Jim a good friend, a mentor, and an inspiration in many ways. This book gave me a front-row seat into his life, personally and professionally. *All Pride, No Ego* is truly authentic, bold, funny, and emotional. A first of its kind. A book anyone interested in the corporate world, or even for those already in leadership positions, should be required to read. *All Pride, No Ego* is 'unputdownable'."

GERARDO CELASCO,
Actor, Producer, Entrepreneur

"Jim has built a tremendous career based on telling stories, and now, lucky for us, he's sharing his own. If you lead a team of humans, read this book."

JILL ROBERTSON,
Co-Founder and CEO, Office

"Inspiring and riveting, *All Pride, No Ego* weaves a fascinating career with wisdom we can all use during these ever-changing times. Jim's journey is a lesson in love, compassion, balance, and evolution, and a compelling reminder to keep our feet on the ground as we reach for the stars."

ELIZABETH LITTEN MILLER,
Former Disney, Dreamworks, and Fox Creative Executive

"I was lucky to experience Jim's leadership firsthand at Disney and at Fox. As an Executive Coach now, I'm thrilled that the world will have access to his insights, wisdom, and actionable career development lessons. Jim is a natural storyteller, and the vulnerability in which he shares how he struggled yet overcame personal and professional challenges is very inspiring. This book should be required reading for students and young professionals interested in succeeding in business roles today while remaining true to their authentic selves."

EVA STEORTZ,
Executive Coach, Marketing Expert and
20 year Disney Executive

.L PRIDE, NO EGO

A Queer Executive's Journey
to Living *and* Leading Authentically

JIM FIELDING

WILEY

Published by John Wiley & Sons, Inc., Hoboken, New Jersey.
Published simultaneously in Canada.

For general information on our other products and services or for technical support, please contact our Customer Care Department within the United States at (800) 762-2974, outside the United States at (317) 572-3993 or fax (317) 572-4002.

Wiley also publishes its books in a variety of electronic formats. Some content that appears in print may not be available in electronic formats. For more information about Wiley products, visit our web site at www.wiley.com.

Library of Congress Cataloging-in-Publication Data:

Names: Fielding, Jim (James D.), author.
Title: All pride, no ego : a queer executive's journey to living and
   leading authentically / Jim Fielding.
Description: Hoboken, New Jersey : John Wiley & Sons, Inc., [2023] |
   Includes index.
Identifiers: LCCN 2023007177 (print) | LCCN 2023007178 (ebook) | ISBN
   9781394165285 (cloth) | ISBN 9781394165308 (adobe pdf) | ISBN
   9781394165292 (epub)
Subjects: LCSH: Fielding, Jim (James D.) | Gay businessmen—United
   States—Biography. | Gay executives—United States—Biography. |
   Gays—United States—Biography. | Success in business. | Success.
Classification: LCC HC102.5.F495 A3 2023 (print) | LCC HC102.5.F495
   (ebook) | DDC 338.092 [B]—dc23/eng/20230223
LC record available at https://lccn.loc.gov/2023007177
LC ebook record available at https://lccn.loc.gov/2023007178

Cover Design: Paul McCarthy
Cover Image: © Getty Images | Arijit Mondal
SKY10049811_062323

This book is dedicated to young people and future leaders globally, especially those questioning how and where they fit in the world.

I will work hard to support and build communities where you can live your full and authentic lives.

Be Happy and Keep Smiling!

Contents

Preface

Hello, Community of Readers, and thank you so much for taking the time to consider this book! *All Pride, No Ego* is about my journey and what shaped my foundational beliefs and leadership style. I did not intend to write an autobiography or a sweeping review of my life, but I have realized that my leadership style and success in my career are completely dependent on my personal journey. I quickly realized that I had to share my successes, failures, and vulnerabilities in order to illustrate why I lead the way I do. I will share anecdotes and episodes, and through sharing and storytelling, I hope to help you achieve whatever your definition of success is for your life. I hope that you see yourself in my story and that regardless of your age, gender, sexual identity, nationality, or profession you learn something useful. I am not sure there has ever really been a book like this. My story is unique, although many of you will recognize pieces of my learnings in your own path. I think it is important for me to share my insights and experiences in an effort to positively impact the world. My learnings and experience may not be applicable to everyone's journey, but I do hope you find this book enjoyable, useful, and thought-provoking. I hope it makes you reflect, learn, and maybe even laugh. If I can help one person find and honor their authentic path in life, I will consider this endeavor a success. I have learned that there is no way to uncouple my leadership style, my creativity, and my professional mistakes from my personal growth, education, and failures. That is what makes me unique. You have vulnerabilities and quirks that make you unique as well. Let's embrace those differences and our authentic stories and change the world. You are never alone, and I am honored to share my learnings and experience with you.

To fully understand my learnings, you will need some foundational information as background and context for what I will share with you. I was born in April 1965 in Toledo, Ohio, at Toledo Hospital. A first-born, Aries, Midwestern male with all of the expectations that accompany these facts. I am the very tippy tail end of being a Baby Boomer, but as a marketer, I can assure you I fully exhibit those traits and expectations normally associated with that demographic. My father was a second-generation firefighter, a military school graduate, an All-state football player, and a Coast Guard veteran. My mother was an x-ray technician, an original latchkey child/child of divorce, and a popular friend to all, who became a stay-at-home housewife when I was born. Both were natives of Toledo, and my extended family was generally in the Toledo area. We attended St. James Church and Sunday dinners at my paternal grandparents weekly.

My beloved sister arrived in 1967, and on the surface, we looked like the perfect, nuclear family. Underneath, our vulnerabilities and dysfunctions were numerous and hidden from public view. We have dealt with addiction, racism, misogyny, homophobia, and a "Fieldings never lie" mantra and myth that would influence my entire life and psyche. I am not sure my parents were each other's great love, but they made it work in their own way.

I felt many expectations, but I also felt like I was given wings and a belief that I would leave home and do something interesting. They just did not realize that they had birthed a complicated unicorn, one who did not naturally fit in traditional societal norms and stereotypes, no matter how hard I tried. And, I tried very hard to fit in. In spite of all this, I did feel love, and I loved my family very much.

I have known I was different, unique, and special since I was 6 years old. I also have known I was gay since then. I did not know what it was called, but I knew I liked boys more than girls (except as friends) and I thought I was broken. I guess this means I have felt "less than" for over 50 years. I went through all of the classic 1980s confusion, guilt, and self-loathing. I wanted to be fixed. I hoped I was bisexual, or that I was in some kind of "phase." I had no one to talk to about my feelings. I had no role models. Therapy was not a common resource. Representation matters! I listened to my family tell horrible racist and homophobic jokes and stories at the dinner table and cocktail parties. I thought gay men were all hairdressers, decorators, or drag queens. If a man in their life was slightly effeminate, he was called fey, or gay, or light in the loafers. I considered surgery to change my voice because I thought I sounded gay. I considered suicide. More than once. I read a lot and listened to a lot of music and I prayed for change. I shoved my feelings down, and I became the "Best Little Boy" I could be. I was competitive, an overachiever, a people pleaser, a joiner, and an excellent student. Why? To prove to myself and anyone else that I was just as good as my straight peers.

I knew I was different and a minority, but I felt I had to show that was only one piece of me. I was not going to let my "deficiency" hold me back from anything. I also knew from a very young age that my future was outside of Toledo, so I needed good grades and activities to gain scholarships and grants to get to a good university. I was president of National Honor Society, German Club, and Senior Class Sargent at Arms. I had many girl friends, several male friends who were my rocks and confidantes, and a bunch of people who did not understand me and just made trouble. In high school, I was voted Most Ambitious, Most Likely To Succeed, Most Preppy, and Biggest Gossip . . . trying to fit in academically and socially. Most Repressed, Depressed, or Conflicted were not voting categories.

Indiana University, Bloomington, and my overseas study in Copenhagen, Denmark, in many ways saved and shaped my life. I will share more of that later in the book, but I know the decision to attend IU and my experiences there allowed me to start the process of loving and understanding myself. Studying political science and business management opened my eyes and mind to global socioeconomics and geopolitics. I had no idea it would be so relevant to my life and chosen path. This period of my life is also when I begin to build my Chosen Family, a group I have loved with, laughed with, and needed for almost 40 years now.

I have enjoyed a long, interesting, and successful career. I was privileged to work with some of the biggest names in retail and media: Millard Drexler, Michael Eisner, Robert Iger, Steve Jobs, Jeffrey Katzenberg, Andy Mooney, Stacey Snider, Ann Daly, Michael Francis, and Amy Nauiokas. All are true innovators and legends, and I am grateful for their guidance and leadership. I also had some "Bad Bosses" and I now understand that sometimes painful experiences and hard-earned wisdom from tough situations is as valuable as what you gain from the superstars.

It is interesting to note, however, that I never had a queer boss or mentor to whom I directly reported. I had queer peers and friends in the industry, and I leaned on that network often, but it does strike me that there was a very visible and impenetrable glass ceiling at times in our industry. I successfully built teams and cultures at very complex and challenging companies and prided myself on managing "diversity" early. I am grateful for everyone who worked with me and allowed me to hone my leadership style through a series of experiments, mistakes, and triumphs. As I grew as a leader, I grew as a person and as a man. I also sacrificed my personal life for professional success, whatever that truly means. I have had four long-term relationships, including one marriage and divorce. I did not have the wisdom to prioritize and balance well early in my life. I was on a mission and had something to prove, mostly to myself. Hindsight is 20/20. I wish someone had shown me my future in a way that allowed me to learn earlier in my life.

Which brings me to this effort. Why a book? Why now? Will anyone actually read my story?

Who cares? I think my leadership style and philosophy are unique and represent an important perspective and voice that is lacking in this genre. There are not a lot of stories or books about Queer Leadership and I believe underrepresented and historically marginalized communities need to be heard. Fundamental human rights are under attack daily. We have lost civility in our social discourse and our democracy. There are rampant mental health issues and impacts, especially in the LBGTQ+ community. Teen suicide is on the rise. There is an appalling lack of mental health services in our schools and communities. Our youth are barraged with instantaneous feedback and attention in this social media world and are not mature enough to handle criticism or separate fact from fiction. Our children have almost unlimited access to information but are losing the ability to truly connect with others in a physical world.

As I write this book, we are slowly emerging into a post Covid-19 world, and I have had periods of isolation and self-reflection. I have watched with increasing anger, horror, and frustration as elected officials attempt to legislate away queer lifestyle and existence, literally forcing human beings to deny their authentic selves and back into the closet. I never imagined my gender identification and/or sexuality would become so politicized. Essentially, by choosing to embrace my authentic self, I have become an activist. I also have been successful in challenging industries like retail and media/entertainment. I worked hard and do not take anything for granted. I want to share my learnings with you to show how anything is possible.

Through all of this and especially throughout the last 5–10 years of my life, I have begun to realize I need to use my voice and platform more effectively to create positive change in the world. I think the freedom of "leaving corporate" has emboldened me and sharpened my senses. I feel renewed and refreshed, and have a heightened awareness of injustice globally. I am keenly focused on the social justice issues of all marginalized voices and communities. Black Lives Matter. Women have a right to choose. Hate crimes against any community scar us a civil society. We all deserve the right to marry. Dictators cannot invade sovereign territories without some kind of swift and decisive response from the global superpowers. We just need to care more. Queer rights are human rights. My homosexuality is my business, and is not a lifestyle choice. But quietly sitting on the sidelines is also not a choice in this environment. We have to love authentically, speak our truth, and address injustice and intolerance. We also have to protect our community from the senseless violence of gay nightclub shooting rampages and the horror of hate violence, especially against the trans community. While some days are better than others, the fight is truly never over.

As I write this, I have watched with horror as the U.S. Supreme Court overturned *Roe v. Wade*. Next, a sitting justice of the same body declares "we" should go after gay marriage and contraception. I have wept with frustration and anger, but it steels my spine to continue with this book and speaking out to support human rights in all forms. The headlines and stories out of Florida and Texas are shameful, frightening, and unbelievable. It feels more like 1960 than 2022, but we all have to face the realities of our current world. We cannot just be angry and frustrated, we must activate and band together to fight this ignorant, hate-filled, and morally bankrupt legislation and rhetoric. Democracy takes work. It is a privilege, not a right, and you must do your part to participate. Do not get lazy and expect others to do the necessary steps to protect you and your family. I will include a list of resources and references at the end of this book if you are looking for ways to get involved locally and in the community.

As I was engaging on this effort, I had some personal insights that I want to share with you. I am a cisgender white male, end of the Baby Boomer generation Buckeye who was born and raised in the industrial Midwest. My family was working upper-middle class, but definitely blue collar in their orientation. We are also proud products of our German, Welsh, and Irish ancestry and heritage. I was taught to find a job that would provide security and stability, which was defined as a guaranteed salary and good benefits, and a pension. The ultimate goals for my generation were very different than for college graduates today. I was taught to be self-reliant and to plan for the worst scenarios, and not rely on anyone for help, especially the government. My family was Reagan Republicans . . . small government, anti-welfare, anti-social safety net, good support for defense and veterans, and let the world take care of its issues. We were taught to dream, but be realistic in our expectations. It was fine to be ambitious, but keep it in check. Success meant a family, kids, working at the same job for 40 years, and retiring with the previously mentioned pension and a watch, and maybe if you were lucky, retiring in Florida to get out of the cold and snow.

Although I now identify as a cis-gender, homosexual, I acknowledge the fact that I benefited from white, male privilege. I realize that made and makes my path easier than many other people, especially my peers in the BIPOC and Trans communities. Still, I did not always feel like my path was challenge free. I did not know anyone whose parents were doctors, lawyers, or CEOS. I did not know the words *start-up* or *entrepreneur*. Nobody worked in tech. I did not know anyone whose Dad owned a company. Our parents were all employees, not bosses. In fact, I watched my Dad struggle with a small company he owned and had inherited from my grandfather. It was called Airways Engineering and was an industrial air conditioning cleaning and maintenance company. Like most firefighters, this was my Dad's side gig to earn more money on his days off from the department. My grandfather had started the business in the 1960s and passed it on to my Dad. He had three workers, an office in our basement, and a separate phone line. He had a checkbook, a ledger, an adding machine, and business cards. I thought it was cool that he was a boss, but I never considered that to be his true calling.

In the late 1970s, I watched his business fall apart, as his major customer, Kresge and Kmart, were sold and decided to centralize their maintenance support to larger operations and national companies. Overnight, his business evaporated and he had to liquidate and lay off people. It never occurred to me to call my Dad a business owner or an entrepreneur. My Dad was a firefighter with a side hustle he did on his days off. I thought it was simply a way to earn more money. Frankly, I never fully understood the emotions of what happened to him and the impact of this closure. I was naïve and self-absorbed, and my Dad was stoic and did not show emotions. He never talked to me about "business," and he never expected me to run it one day.

A lot of my business world innocence and naïveté is a result of when and where I was born. Toledo, Ohio, was directly linked to Detroit, Michigan, and the auto industry. Any impacts on the domestic auto industry (gas prices, oil crisis, foreign imports, union battles) caused dramatic fluctuations in our economy and lives. I spent one semester of elementary school going to school from 1 p.m. to 7 p.m., as our school was closed due to the cost of heating oil and other utilities. That meant we had to "share" one of the remaining open schools, and we were bussed daily for our afternoon shift. The only kids I knew who went to private school were the Catholic kids, and it was solely about a religious education, not about college preparation.

Our public high school counselors focused on truancy, delinquency, and kids who were failing. There was no college preparation training or standardized test study programs. We did not even have a college fair night! Since my parents had not gone away for college, I learned about various universities and colleges from the brochures mailed to my house after I took the PSAT.

I was lucky that some of my older friends who graduated before me did go away for school, so I was able to watch and learn from them. I visited them on campus during my junior and senior year of high school and that was really my first exposure to "going away for school." For a variety of reasons, I knew I needed good grades, activities, and letters of recommendation to "get out."

My dear friend Amanda was one year ahead of me, and she was (and still is) a role model for me. I tried to do everything she did to get the scholarships and the advice on choosing the right school. Amanda taught me about the importance of balancing a passion for arts, humanities, and the sciences. She also educated me on class ranking, preparing for standardized tests, and opening my mind to schools everywhere. We also laughed a lot and saw a lot of movies together. We ate way too many late-night breakfast buffets and danced with joy and abandon. Amanda was my built-in school dance partner, the smartest person I knew, and wise way beyond her years. When I saw her graduate at the top of her class and go to an elite all-girls' college in Virginia, she literally changed my life. I met Amanda when I was 13 years old and love her like a sister still today.

I was convinced I wanted to go to an Ivy League school, especially Princeton, probably from watching movies or reading articles somewhere. In the end, I was too intimidated to even finish the application, as my inner voice stunted my ambition. I had not gone to a prep school. I was not a legacy. I was not from a wealthy family that had a family office or a trust set up for me. I was so insecure in so many ways, not just about my sexuality. Do not get me wrong. I am not judging anyone who was born into a different situation or created their own opportunities and had a different path. In fact, I am jealous and I wish I had some guidance and wisdom bestowed upon me along the way. At times, I felt like an explorer, and I made a lot of mistakes. I hopefully learned from all of them. I think these facts are why I work so hard to help others find their path and enable them to see what is possible with an education.

Why am I sharing all of this? It is not for any honor and glory for being a self-made man. I do not actually think I am that different from many of my friends and peers who grew up at the same time as I did. It is to show you that anything is possible and that the American dream did exist for me. At times, I assumed the world was against me, as I was "different," but I forged ahead. My hard work, natural talents, eagerness to learn, and some good mentors along the way made me who I am today.

I am saying this because I realize I had to overcome two sets of insecurities and self-perceptions. The first was my socioeconomic background and family position. The second was my sexuality and sexual identity. I realize now that I was basically running to overcome both real and imagined deficiencies. I think that is why I sometimes felt as if I were on a never-ending treadmill, just trying to keep up. I am not stronger than anyone else I know. I am not more lucky or more strategic. I have always tried to navigate this world honestly and with hard work, and I feel like I have been rewarded with an interesting life and a diverse set of experiences and friends as a result.

As I said before, my life is not a guideline or rule book for anyone else, but I do hope I can share some learnings that may feel like a bit of road map for some people. I also hope I can encourage people to stay open-minded and open-eyed to new opportunities and insights. You never really know what is possible until it happens. I also hope that readers learn to ask for help when needed and realize it is much easier to build your definition of a successful life with support and a community.

Reading *Caste* by Isabel Wilkerson and *How to Be an Antiracist* by Ibram X. Kendi was also an awakening for me and spurred me to this exercise of self-discovery and sharing. My work and education in the Diversity, Equity, and Inclusion space has been fascinating and daunting. I was struck how a poli-sci major and a history buff had somehow missed these types of teachings and insights they shared in my curriculum. I realized there was a caste system that existed as I was coming up in the world, and the caste system I was put into as a gay man when I came out was real. I am not remotely trying to compare my experience to that of a BIPOC individual, but I do empathize and understand more now than ever in my life. It is tiring, overwhelming, and frustrating to go through life and a career as an "other." It is important to acknowledge visible and invisible differences. While I present initially as a white male when I enter a room, I have invisible differences that have in many ways marginalized me before I even begin. I think this is another reason I chose this writing project.

The theme of my 1983 high school graduation speech to the Whitmer National Honor Society was "May we leave our corner of the world a little better than we found it." Forty odd years later, I share this work with you following that same sentiment. I wish I had a book like this when I was starting out in my career. I wish the scared and lonely teenager and young man that I was had someone share a book like this with him. I wish I could go back and try some things over! I hope everyone takes one new insight away after spending time with my story and learnings. I hope you more quickly define happiness, fulfillment, and success than I did. I would be honored to support any journey to your personal truth, leading authentically, and living with joy and satisfaction. Live out loud! Keep smiling! Love yourself!

Find someone to love and be loved unconditionally! Please know I am rooting for you every day and I cannot wait to see and feel your impact on your community and the world. We all need your authentic power and contributions.

As I have not written this book in chronological order, I am going to share a brief timeline overview of my career with you now as an orientation and a guide for my stories:

1965	Born in Toledo, Ohio
1983	Graduated Whitmer High School, Toledo, Ohio
Spring 1986	Overseas Study (Denmark International Studies), Copenhagen, Denmark
1987	Graduated Indiana University, B.A. Political Science with Outside Field in Business Administration, Bloomington, Indiana
1987–1989	Dayton Hudson Department Store Company, Minneapolis, Minnesota; Flint, Michigan; and Detroit, Michigan
1989–1998	Gap, Inc., Detroit, Michigan; Chicago, Illinois; and San Francisco, California
1998–1999	J. Peterman Company, Lexington, Kentucky
1999–2001	Lands' End, Madison, Wisconsin
2001–2012	The Walt Disney Company, Los Angeles, California
2001–2002	VP, Merchandise Disney Catalog
2002–2004	SVP, Merchandise Disney Store
2004–2008	SVP and EVP, Retail Sales and Marketing, Disney Consumer Products
2008–2012	President, Disney Stores Worldwide

2012–2014	CEO, Claire's Stores, Inc., Chicago, Illinois
2014–2015	SVP, Consumer Products Awesomeness TV, Los Angeles, California
2015– 2017	Global Head, Consumer Products Dreamworks, Los Angeles, California
2017–2019	President, Consumer Products and Experiences, 20th Century Fox Studios and Television, Los Angeles, California
2019–2020	Partner, Then What, Inc., Beverly Hills, California
2020–Present	President, Archer Gray Co-Lab, New York, New York (based in Atlanta, Georgia)
2021–2023	Executive-in-Residence (part-time), Indiana University, Bloomington, Indiana

And now I give you *All Pride, No Ego*. . . . Let's go on a leadership and personal growth journey, and thank you for caring enough to spend some time with me.

1

Control the Controllable, but Leave Space for the Possible

Anyone who has worked with me in the last 25 years has heard me say this phrase multiple times. It has become a mantra of sorts for me and the teams I have led. It is applicable to many situations, both personal and professional. When you work in retail and media/entertainment, you use it often, as the pace of change can be frightening.

I have always been a very firm believer in fate. I am spiritual and believe in the power of prayer and the presence of a Higher Power. I was raised with the guidance of the Golden Rule "Do unto others as you would have them do unto you." I was raised in a family that valued intelligent discussion, participating in your community, and giving back to those less fortunate than you. I was also raised with the simple idea that hard work and patience will be rewarded, although no one ever fully defined the reward to me, or correctly for my life.

While I believe in fate and destiny to an extent, I have never felt like a victim or a bystander waiting and watching for something impactful to occur in my life. In fact, I firmly believe the Fates have multiple scenarios in their plans for us. You are presented options and decisions, and how you choose those inflection points will guide your journey. We have choice. We have control. You just need to learn how much and how to use it wisely. If you haven't seen an amazing movie called *The Adjustment Bureau*, starring Matt Damon and Emily Blunt, I highly endorse a viewing. It actually examines and explains my personal drive and belief system very accurately. I watch it often and learn something new every time.

The harsh reality of my Type-A, compulsive, and overzealous control freak behavior for much of my life is that I am a classic

Adult Child of an Alcoholic (ACOA). I was raised in an active alcoholic household. My mother suffered with the disease my entire life, finally entering a rehabilitation program on my 39th birthday. We had severe and regular episodes of "Mom's sickness." Vodka was her demon. Ironically, vodka is my spirit of choice, although I am not a very big drinker. As the first-born and Mom's favorite boy, I learned at a very young age how to help her, how to cope, and how never to discuss or disclose the situation. I felt it was my job to protect my younger sister from the disease's impact. The disease drove a wedge between me and my Dad, because I wanted him to "fix" and handle the situation. I felt he ignored the situation and did not listen to her or try to learn her patterns and triggers.

As I got older, and after much therapy, I realize my Dad was practicing "detachment" and actually held the family together during these episodes. That is advanced reasoning for a nine-year-old whose Mom is passed out on Christmas Eve with the family arriving in three hours and a frozen turkey and unbaked ham. I was thrust into adult situations and decisions way too early. I think that is part of the reason I forgot how to just be a child. I also realize it taught me how to operate in crisis mode and anticipate situations before they materialize. I developed a sixth sense for my Mom's triggers, and I would prepare myself and my sister mentally for what I could see coming. That skill has translated into my career. I know I have an ability to read situations and synthesize information quickly, sometimes too fast! My executive coach told me I needed to be careful because I would assess a situation so fast sometimes that I would not let the group I was working with the natural time they needed to catch up, and I could show frustration on my face. By the way, I am a horrible poker player; I wear my emotions on my face and others can easily see the quality of my hand. Same issue with my leadership feelings: I am an open book.

My maternal grandmother (Grandma Shabby—because I could not say Shirley) tried to help me in her own way. When I was 11, she gave me a card with the Serenity Prayer on it. "God grant me the Serenity to accept the things I cannot change, the Courage to change the things I can, and the Wisdom to know the difference." I still have that card tucked away somewhere in my memory boxes. It took me 20 years to know the prayer was part of the 12-step recovery community. In typical fashion, she gave the me the card with no context or conversation. I guess she figured I was smart enough to learn from it and understand my Mom's situation.

Typical of my family, we would just not talk about difficult topics. I was not that wise or self-aware yet, and I wish I was stronger to ask for help and insights. Instead, I developed advance coping skills and control mechanisms. I also started to develop my alternative narrative techniques, an advanced storytelling skill that managed the truth and moved focus away from facts. Basically, we kept Mom's disease in the closet. Please understand, this was not a daily occurrence, but it happened often enough to become a pattern of behavior and rehearsed responses. Technically, I think she was a called an episodic alcoholic, but I am not an expert on the disease. Not that the term made it easier, but at least it had a name. As I got older, I could start to see the patterns more clearly and sense when a storm was coming. At times, I tried to divert my Mom's pain and make her work on something, or more importantly, make her laugh. When that did not work, I shifted to overtime to shield my sister and to lay as low as possible.

I could not love my Mom more, and I truly understand her pain and the disease now. I have studied, and read, and listened to groups, and learned about the clinical side of addiction. I have met so many people who have struggled with it on their own and in their own families. I admire people who have succeeded in their own recovery processes and work in sober communities to help others. To me, having and being a sponsor is the ultimate sign of mentorship and mental health. I am glad I am at this point in my life, where I can now look back and study the learnings and situations. Regardless, it was very painful and I spent a lot of my youth as a scared little boy. It is, however, a major part of my authenticity and story. These childhood realities have driven my leadership style and my personal life dramatically and that is why I chose to start my shared learnings with this subject area.

Early in my life, I became a neat freak, almost to an OCD-type level of behavior. I could not and still cannot stand clutter of any kind . . . on kitchen counters, in drawers, on shelves in my office. "Junk drawers" make me break out in a cold sweat. Container Store was developed solely for me. Oh, the joy of translucent boxes in all shapes and sizes that place can bring out in me! I hate surprises, even on my birthday. I operate better with a plan. No one would ever call me spontaneous. I have attempted to look forward and anticipate next moves since I was seven or eight years old.

Ironically, I was rewarded for that early in my career, as I was seen as proactive and visionary. I was encouraged to be independent and take initiative. My bosses had no idea I had been preparing myself for these roles and various scenarios my entire life by managing my family dynamics. I walked on eggshells as a child and became very risk-averse. I ALWAYS colored within the lines. I was and am a rule follower. I was afraid to confront, disappoint, or have a conflict with anyone, and was told early in my management career that I actively avoided tough conversations.

It also affected my ability to talk directly to my partners about relationships. However, I was also very quick to show my temper, and could throw a mean tantrum. I would let things build up over time and then pop off, and it is not a pretty trait. Teachers loved me because I always volunteered to clean erasers, sharpen pencils, or read aloud, or gather the other kids for recess. I was dependable, reliable, and always received excellent marks for my citizenship. I thrived on consistency and positive feedback. I needed to be the best or the favorite. I loved order and predictability, and anything out of the norm created stress and nerves. I won the school spelling bee a few times. I joined Cub Scouts and even got a trophy for the Pinewood Derby.

You see, I was doing anything to keep my parents and family, and most especially my Mom, happy and "normal." I naïvely thought that if I excelled at everything and made them happy and proud, I could control her drinking episodes. I thought if I did typical boy things like Scouts and sports that my Dad would love me more. I thought he was amazing and I just wanted to be more like him. I was very aware that I was not really the son he expected, even though he never said anything like that aloud. I felt it deeply though. It gnawed at me pretty consistently. I learned early, however, that he admired and appreciated success, so I doubled down on winning his approval, and ultimately, his love through achievements. In adulthood, I learned I was seeking something special and elusive called unconditional love and acceptance. I also learned that if I had been stronger at an early age and just talked openly and honestly, my life may have been very different with my parents. Oh, how I wish I would have had the power to see the future.

I know now that I was living a double life since a very early age, oddly preparing me for life as a closeted gay man. I was learning how to compartmentalize and lock emotions down internally, while presenting a wholesome and happy image publicly. I remember hearing a story about swans and how they are serene and calm above the surface, but they are powerfully moving their legs underneath the water. I think I mastered swan-like behavior out of necessity, but that does not mean I was happy. I spent much of my youth, and especially my adolescence, in a spiral of self-loathing, confusion, and almost desperate hunt for approval and validation from others, especially adult authority figures and the "popular" kids at school.

I find it interesting how this "control freak" trait manifested itself in my early career. I entered a department store executive training program upon college graduation in 1987. My Dad drove with me to Minneapolis, Minnesota, in June—four weeks after leaving Bloomington.

By the way, I was dating a woman at this point in my life and had just broken up with the man I was dating throughout senior year of college. Control mechanisms in full swing, as I convinced myself I was bisexual. Unable to accept the life I pictured as a queer, I convinced myself to suppress feelings and be "normal." I wanted to get married, to have children, to buy a house with a white picket fence. In 1987, that only happened with a traditional marriage between a man and a woman, especially in the Midwest. I truly loved the woman I was dating, but more like a warm friendship. I just assumed I could tamp down my latent sexuality and "make it work." I wanted my parents to be happy grandparents. I wanted my friends to still love being around me. I thought I had it all under wraps and under control. How silly was that?

I chose the retail industry as a temporary two-year stopover on my way to law school or a master's in international business.

I entered day one of the training program and quickly identified my competition for the coveted placements at the end of 90 days training. I dove headfirst into the classes and the practical floor training. I studied materials at night and on my breaks. I was determined to be the "best." I learned that "retail is detail" and I had a knack for customer service and merchandising. I rose quickly in the program and was offered a permanent placement as the Men's Claiborne and Contemporary Collection Selling Manager in the flagship store downtown and I never looked back. I also never considered law school any more. I was good at my job and I was receiving external praise and validation.

I was also exploring the gay nightlife scene in Minneapolis and I was stunned to learn that there were professional, successful queer people in all kinds of jobs and professions. At work, however, I was firmly in the closet. This was the late 1980s. It was the height of the AIDS epidemic and hysterical ignorance that came with this disease. The impact and the rumors were felt throughout the queer community. I was in fear of discovery of the truth and how it would impact my career. I was in a relationship, but I turned "him" into "they" and was very careful about never really talking about my personal life. I just kept it all separate and thought I had it hidden and under control. He was older than I was and he worked part-time at the store, so it was really taboo.

I got promoted to a store in Flint, Michigan. Not only did I have to hide my sexuality, but I also was asked to hide the fact that I was only 23 years old and that I would be managing people in their 40s and 50s. I also hid the fact that my "room-mate" from Minneapolis decided to move to Flint as well, seemingly for no reason. So many secrets. It felt very heavy. I was constantly on edge. I put my head down and doubled me efforts at success, as I saw promotion out of that store as my only possible path. I did get promoted to a Detroit-area store, but it was more of the same. I had an amazing store manager, though, who knew my truth and kept it confidential. I also met other closeted queer managers, and we formed a some-what secret social group for our weekends and free evenings. It is so tiring leading a double life on so many levels. It was overly stressful and I began to experience physical issues like migraine headaches and stomach ailments. Never underestimate the physical, emotional, and mental toll that hiding your true self takes on your life.

For my queer community friends of my generation, you will recognize much of this chapter of my life. The 1980s were dev-astating for our community. Growing up gay in the AIDS crisis was overwhelming. Even if you were lucky enough to find someone to love, you lived in constant fear of the disease and its wrath. You felt like our community was being punished for being our true selves. People hated us, were afraid of us, and actively worked to ostracize us. Most people equated gay with AIDS, and ultimately, with death. As a young queer, I did not feel strong enough to confront all of this, and I was increasingly more depressed and physically ill. Something had to change.

It was at this point I realized I needed to "come out," both personally and professionally, so I could control and own my narrative and be "healthy." My darling sister, Jill, somewhat forced the personal process by asking my "roommate" to be in her wedding and giving me a deadline to tell our parents, as I was forcing her to lie in a family who did not lie to each other. I think that was a common story in the 1980s and 1990s for many families and their queer members . . . it often divided a family and forced dysfunctional secret keeping.

I shared my truth with my mother while she was driving around 70 mph on I-75 in suburban Toledo. We were in town for a family reunion picnic at my aunt and uncle's farm, and my sister was pushing me pretty hard to own my story. I sat in the passenger seat and tears formed in my eyes. My Mom asked what was wrong, and I literally pushed on my stomach to get the words out. Basically, I had to metaphorically vomit out the truth. "Mom, I am gay." Instantly, I felt release and burst into full tears. My Mom said, "I have known, and I just was waiting for you to tell me. It was not my place to ask." She pulled over to the side of the road, hugged me, and we talked for about an hour. My Mom accepted my story and seemed oddly prepared for the conversation, thanks to Phil Donahue and Oprah Winfrey viewing. I can only imagine how hard it was for her to wait for my news. I am grateful she did not push me.

My Mom and I agreed to tell Dad slowly and at the "right time." I was planning on visiting them in Florida, where they had retired, for his birthday in September and decided to have the conversation on that trip. In August, I came home from work, and my partner told me to listen to the answering machine messages. My Mom had called and basically said "I told your Dad and I think you had better call him." My heart sank to my stomach. I began to sweat. I was nauseated. I picked up the phone that moment and dialed them. Dad answered and promptly hung up on me. I cried for an hour and shook uncontrollably. Everything I had been telling myself was coming true. He did not love me. He could not love me because I was broken and bad, because I am gay.

So began my one-year odyssey with my Dad. He refused to talk to me, but he would send me long typed letters regularly, telling me how I was making a bad choice and it was going to ruin my life. He suddenly became very religious and was quoting biblical references and interpretations. There were vague mentions of Adam and Eve, not Adam and Steve. I knew what he was saying and doing, and it hurt so much. I feel the most critical relationship a boy has is with his father. It has the potential to be simultaneously wonderful, affirming, and scarring. I was devastated and an emotional wreck at home. Remember, however, this is a control the controllable story . . . and I excelled at work. I poured all my anger and insecurities into work and I made a "moment of truth" decision.

Now that I had acknowledged my personal story, I could no longer work for a company that would not allow me to be my full, authentic self at work. I accepted a district manager in training role with the Gap and was fully open and present throughout my interview process. Every person I interviewed with was gracious and calm and supportive. In fact, their leadership had recruited me for my skill set and my track record. I saw that my personal life was not an even issue or consideration. No one at Gap asked me to be anything except the best version of me. Unconditional acceptance is wonderful and made me want to perform for them. So, the lesson is . . . find a company whose ethics and values align with your own. To give a company your best, you need to bring ALL of you to the role every day, and not dissect yourself into acceptable and unacceptable parts.

That moment of truth was one of the best decisions in my early career. It also gave me the confidence to fly to Florida after one year of distance to have it out with my Dad. Guess what? It was not easy, but it worked. I knew it was a make-or-break moment for our relationship. I honestly felt like I did not have a choice; there was no turning back. He was beginning to understand I was still his son and his first-born. I think he was starting to realize I was building a career successfully and maybe who I loved was irrelevant, as long as I was loved. I think what clinched the reconciliation was his acceptance of the fact that I was doing well in my career and people were not holding me back due to my queerness. He was oddly protecting me, in reality. He admitted he was worried about me being bullied or held back, and I flashed back to our non-conversations in high school, which I will share later in this book. I had accepted this kind of love and acceptance from him my whole life, but I have to say it felt like I lost 50 pounds that day. I had no excuses and nothing holding me back at work or home anymore.

Another example of a control the controllable moment was when I became president of Global Disney Stores in May 2008. Andy Mooney, the head of Consumer Products and my boss since 2001, had me work on a "secret project" beginning in fall 2007. Our licensee for the Disney Stores in North America wanted out of its long-term license agreement that had been negotiated under the Michael Eisner–era leadership team. Disney was now led by Robert Iger, with Steve Jobs of Apple fame as the largest individual shareholder and a board member due to the Pixar acquisition. It was a new day, and there was a new appreciation for the global brand importance and impact of the Disney Stores.

I worked with a very small team of smart people to present three options to the board of directors: 1) license the stores to a new entity, 2) allow the stores to close completely in North America, or 3) bring them back into the company as a wholly owned subsidiary of Consumer Products and form a global team. I worked very hard to present a fact-based and unbiased overview of all three options, but I had my favorite. The board agreed to bring the stores back into the company, and overnight, we formed the Global Disney Store team with me as president and operations based in Los Angeles, London, and Tokyo.

I had never worked so hard in my life or had as much passion for what we were doing and recreating. We worked seven days a week, but we were committed to doing it better and more innovative than had been done in the past. I felt the full support of Andy, Bob, and Steve. We were honored to fly to Cupertino to meet with Steve and his retail team in person to listen and learn about their successful, global retail roll-out. They shared everything they had learned about their physical store strategy. One key learning was to build a functional laboratory where you could experiment and learn before committing to the final concept. We were granted the time and budget to build a fully operational, full-size prototype of the new store design and experience. We built a world-class team of talent, bringing in the best and brightest global merchant minds and operators. We reinvented the product, the branding, the customer service model, the packaging, and the culture. We created magical moments and elements of surprise and delight throughout the experience. As my father would have said, "We were cooking with gas." I was so happy and motivated, and would wake up at night to write notes to remember the next day as we pushed ourselves to create something never seen before and worthy of the Disney brand.

We were 90 days into the project when the housing crisis and global recession began in fall 2008. Our business instantly dropped off by almost half. The global economy was tanking. Consumer spending, especially on discretionary items or categories (like Disney Store) fell off a cliff. We all felt a sense of panic and dread and had a lack of clarity of what was really happening and how long it would last. This is when I knew we had to "take control of what we could." Misery loves company, and our entire world and industry were dealing with the same issues, but that did not give us a hall pass at Disney. It was another "moment of truth" in my journey; I had a choice to use excuses or to surf the disruptions. I chose to surf and stay positive.

We stayed focused on the fact that families would try to protect or shield children from the effects of the recession. There were still birthdays and Christmas and Hanukkah and elementary school graduations to celebrate, and we needed to bring the magic. I was grateful the team wanted to surf with me and embrace problem solving and solution discovery. We did everything we could think of to control expenses and protect earnings. It created a fiscal discipline culture that stayed with us after the crisis and helped us turn around the gross revenue and operating income to historic highs. I will write more about my time at Disney Stores in this story, but I can share that this role was my favorite in my career and life. Bringing magic to families and children around the world with our focus on the "best 30 minutes of their day" was a privilege and an honor. Do not misunderstand, I also never worked harder in my life. It was all-consuming and required a 24/7 focus, but the magical moments made it all worthwhile. Most importantly, we had a global team that was working at the same level of intensity and creativity I was, and that was so special. To this day, whenever I run into some cast member from that period, we discuss it fondly. That amazes me. As I reflect, I am so proud of what that team was able to accomplish in the face of tremendous adversity and daily change. The work we did on "Plush Mountain" and on expanding the costumes and role-play business is still evident today when you walk into the parks or go online. It was such a team effort and a shared commitment to surprising and delighting our guests. I can still see our team's impact when I enter the flagship stores around the world. It amazes me that I still get recognized by cast members in the stores, and as I look around, I can see the light touches of magic that we tried to bring back to the physical retail experience.

I could write a separate book on "how" we turned around the Disney Store business and guest experience during that 2008–2012 period (and maybe I will!). For the young leaders just starting out, here are some key learnings that you may find useful in your own career journey. 1) Set a clear mission and vision for your business, and establish both qualitative and quantitative goals that can be measured over time. Ensure that everyone on your team is clear about those goals and their role in achieving them. 2) Recruit, train, and retain the best and brightest people in the industry. Hire people who are smarter than you are, and let them fly. 3) Get to know everyone on your team and celebrate all accomplishments and key events. Commit to quality, innovation, and authentic storytelling in your product and excellent customer service always. Our cast members (employees) consistently exceeded expectations, and I would hear about it from tweets, social media posts, and letters. Our guests, our fans, our customers were always #1 and they knew they had direct access to me and my leadership team around the world. There is a funny story about accessibility from that period that I would like to share. I started a Twitter account called "DisneyStorePrez" early on in my tenure as a way of sharing news and social listening. Smart fans started to direct message me and test if it was really me answering or if I had delegated the work to the marketing team. It got a little out of control when I would tweet that I was visiting a certain store or market and people would show up to talk to me in person. Disney corporate security did not like that at all! I, however, loved it and felt like I was getting pure, unfiltered feedback from our guests. That is one of the things I love about retail. You receive a report card every morning and can react to the results. There is so much more to share, but again, I am very grateful to the team that was on the journey and turnaround with me.

I grew tremendously as a leader and as a person. I grew in confidence and a belief in my decision-making abilities. I worked to overcome my conflict avoidant nature and my negative internal self-talk. I learned what I could truly control, and I learned how to roll with the punches and the unexpected. I learned to not be derailed by surprises and negative events. I learned how to not "over" react or "over" correct. Again, there were moments I blew it. I would "lose it" often, to the point of my HR head, Peter, needing to take me for walks to calm down. He was and is a truth teller! What you need to understand is that I had to make mistakes in order to learn and grow. That was probably the biggest gift—I learned I did not have to be PERFECT to be successful. I also learned that I had a team of excellence who would perform wonderfully and I did not have to do it all alone.

I want to end the learning section of this chapter explaining what I mean by the chapter title . . . control the controllable, but leave space for the possible.

My leadership style and philosophy is guided by my own 80/20 rule. I believe that if I plan and anticipate 80% of my work plan or strategy, and in reality, my life, and execute well, the 20% of surprises and change will be handled more successfully and efficiently by me and my team. I could handle surprises and bad news if I had a solid fundamental plan in place.

This is what I am most excited about at this point in my career. I actually look forward to the 20% with zeal and glee. It is like Christmas morning to me—that joy of anticipation mixed with surprise and delight. The reality is that the world, the consumer, the marketplace, and technology are changing at a pace that I do not think any of us anticipated. Any leader who tells you they have it nailed is a liar. No one has a crystal ball or a magic pill to take that gives you so much wisdom and foresight. Yes, there are smart people in the world, and futurists whom I admire, but for the average leader, you have to keep your mind and energy open for the unexpected. I now love the art of the possible. I always will be a planner. I can almost hear my family, my partner, and people who have worked with me laughing at this passage, but it is true. I am better today than I have ever been at going with the flow, but I wish completely I had learned that in my 30s instead of my 50s.

I firmly believe I have worked hard to earn wisdom and experience, and I remain committed to controlling the controllable, as I can confirm that makes me a successful businessperson and leader. BUT please understand, I now know you must keep a balance. If you attempt to control too much, you will drive yourself and your teams crazy. Most importantly, you may miss key new learnings and opportunities if you are too controlling and close-minded. The pace of innovation and change is faster than I have ever seen in my life. At Disney, I worked with a very talented executive named Luis Fernandez, who was the head of our creative team. He created many opportunities for our team to express their personal creativity and innovation and always encouraged people to think outside our four walls. His talent and style were the perfect complement to my approach, and he stretched me to be more spontaneous and open to newness. He also showed me that good ideas are everywhere if you just open your eyes and ears.

I love the Chinese proverb "When the winds of change blow, there are those who build walls and those who build windmills." I hope I am a windmill builder and I encourage you to try to build some as well. My current work life is a series of interesting projects and clients, many of which I found by staying open and connected to my network, almost "happy accidents" in a way. I am grateful for the opportunity to work on a diverse set of projects and companies. Advising and consulting keeps me sharp, current, and pushes me to not only use my experience, but also learn new insights and skills. I will change gears someday, but now I want my entire mind and body firing on all cylinders. I tell friends that a key word for me is *VITAL*. I just want to be vital. And I always want to be full of pride and remain humble. No one is perfect. No one is always right. The key is to do your best and learn and grow from your missteps. Failing forward is a skill that can be learned over time with healthy experimentation. Learn when to control, when to let go, and the wisdom to know the difference and you will be much more calm and happy than I was for most of my life.

2 | Be a Lifelong Learner and Stay Constantly Curious

I think the first gift I remember as a child was a Dr. Seuss book. I was obsessed with reading from a very young age and continue to read daily now. I tried e-readers, but I love the feel and smell and visceral reaction I have to a physical book. I always look for independent bookstores when I travel . . . I enjoy the sense of wonder and discovery. I also love the smells, the light, and the history of old bookstores. I will read books, magazines, newspapers, and any other form of written knowledge. I devoured The Hardy Boys series, Nancy Drew, and Agatha Christie mysteries as a kid, and now enjoy historical fiction, espionage thrillers, and contemporary novels. I also delight in self-help books and "business" books, and always try to digest learnings from biographies and autobiographies of interesting people. I was blessed to be born into an extended family of readers. Everyone in my family was always carrying around some type of book. My paternal grandmother read every day until her death at 101. Both of my grandfathers were incredible storytellers. My maternal grandfather even came outfitted with props for his stories. Some of my fondest memories with him revolve around Dillinger the Pig and his adventure, which Grandpa told with small pewter figurines he had procured. When we gathered for family dinners, the discussion always included current events, neighborhood gossip, and a review of your current book selections. I think the love of literature is a very important gift that all children should be exposed to at an early age. It opens the imagination and stretches the brain in fascinating ways. It also teaches what is possible. It exposes children to so many adventures, and new places, and new cultures, and sometimes just a funny new story.

This early and lifelong love of reading leads me to my second insight to share.

Never stop learning. Never stop listening. Stay constantly curious.

It scares and saddens me when people think they are done learning. The world is constantly evolving and changing at such a rapid pace now. The consumer marketplace is never done changing. Competition comes and goes daily. Technology has altered everything about how we communicate, interact, receive and digest information, shop, and consume content.

As a leader, you have a need to stay informed, stay open-minded, and interpret trends for your company and team. You need to challenge yourself and your team and your peers and your boss to embrace innovation, new ideas and technologies, and challenges to the status quo. You never change just for the sake of saying you have changed, but you must adapt to stay relevant. It is difficult, but you need to understand that change is inevitable, and if you embrace change and learn how to use knowledge and experience to react to the change positively, you will become an invaluable resource to your organization. I am a change agent, and I am always looking for other change agents. I was also the "fixer upper" at many of my companies because I like puzzles and problem solving.

My leadership philosophy and expectations around change management goes something like this: think of change as a train on a platform at a station.

The train is leaving the station for a new destination. You have a choice to make. You can get on the engine car and drive the change. If you choose the first-class seats or second-class compartment, you can positively participate and frame the change and assume a lead role. If you jump on the luggage car, you can support the change as a valued team player. If you are caboose joiner, we welcome you on the team and will have an important role for you. You may also stand on the track and wave as the train departs the station, but then you are a victim of the change. You choose where to get on the train. I admire anyone who gets on the train, but I especially like the engineers and early travelers. I also understand if you choose another mode of transportation or another destination, but the change is inevitable and will impact you, whether you ride the train or not.

Not everyone will handle change the same or accept it at the same pace. I understand that being a change agent leader is about helping people through inevitable periods of change. It does not have to be overly stressful for teams if you try to help. Simply acknowledging the change and owning your own vulnerabilities and insecurities around the change are sometimes the key that lead to breakthrough moments for your team.

There are also two phrases that I dislike as a leader, especially in times of change. Both are two typical responses to the question "Why do we do it this way?" Anytime I moved into a new role, this was a key question I would ask of my new team.

The change-killer responses are:

1. "We have always done it this way. . . ."
2. "We tried something like that before and it did not work. . . ."

These phrases are just so close-minded and shut down any communication or collaboration possibilities. I am not saying people on our teams do not have the right to question and struggle with change, but I am simply asking them to try to learn a new way of doing something or thinking. It is a problem for my leadership style if you present as a problem identifier, rather than a solution provider. Again, everyone is entitled to their own opinions and their own pace of handling change, but at some point, you have to move forward. Leading those efforts can be challenging, but also rewarding.

Examples from my career where I embraced my learning skills and curiosity are numerous and varied. Lifelong learning is a common theme in my career, and I am still learning every day.

In 1993, I was a district manager for the Gap running the Chicago Northwest area. I enjoyed the city, the company, our team, and my peer group very much. I thought I was on a career path to be a regional manager and then a zone vice president or more. I was a "field" person focused on customer service, flawless visual presentation, and stacking product "High to watch it Fly." We were completely KPI-oriented and goal-focused. This was the heady era of the Gap when America was very uniform-oriented in fashion apparel. These were the days when your pocket T table could sell out in one week, and groups of teens roamed their local malls on weekends and after school. My stores always looked clean, organized, and full. I prided myself on recruiting, training, developing, and retaining excellent managers.

One week, we hosted Millard (Mickey) Drexler and his senior team for a series of store visits in Chicago. Mickey was the brilliant "merchant prince" of specialty retail and the CEO of Gap Inc. We were in a budget-conscious phase, so rather than renting a van, we drove the corporate executives in our company cars. Mickey was in my car, which meant I was "on" for the entire visit. Shortly after that visit, my boss called me and said, "Mickey thinks you are a merchant." I honestly did not even know what a "merchant" was or that merchandising was a verb or a career. The product development team was based in San Francisco and was a talented, yet distant and separate crew. I had never considered that I had any skills in this specialty. My boss encouraged me to visit San Francisco for a week to attend "Line Review" and meet some people. Of course, I leapt at the chance for a free trip to SF! If anything, it was a learning opportunity that would help me do my current and future roles better.

For a little gay boy from Toledo, San Francisco was Disneyland or Oz. It only existed in dreams and movies. I arrived and instantly fell in love with the city. I went to the Castro (the gay district) and felt at home in my tribe.

Then, I entered Gap HQ at 1 Harrison Street and was overwhelmed with the possibilities. The team was smart, passionate, savvy, charming, and everyone seemed gorgeous and to be doing important work. I remember distinctly that there was a kind of uniform . . . white shirts and jeans or denim shirts and khakis, and yet everyone accessorized in a way that made it uniquely their own. They talked in a language I had never heard before . . . merchant speak. They were literally deciding what America (and the world) would be wearing in 12–18 months, and I was fascinated. On Day 3, I knew I wanted to be a merchant. Remember, this chapter is about committing to lifelong learning. I had no idea what I was doing, but in six weeks I had moved from Chicago to San Francisco, bought a convertible, and moved into the Castro. I was a proud gay man living in the best city in the world, working for one of the world's leading retail companies. What could possibly go wrong?

In short, everything! I went from feeling like a confident and focused field executive with a defined career path to being a trainee overnight. I instantly felt stupid, like the slowest reader and learner in a classroom. This was not a familiar feeling. Working at the Gap in the 1990s was like getting an MBA in retail excellence. I shared an office with future CEOs and presidents like Maureen Chiquet (Old Navy and Chanel), Ken Pilot (Polo), Reenie Benziger (Nike and Orvis), and Tom Kennedy (Fossil and Sperry). I was so insecure, I would take work home at night to study and prepare for daily work and meetings. Presenting to Mickey Drexler was a terrifying tight rope walk, but he made you better every time. He made you know and understand every aspect of your business.

As I started to achieve my footing, I realized that I loved what I was doing, and I was enjoying the learning and growth process. I went across the USA to learn how denim was made. Denim fabric was milled in South Carolina from local cotton, which was then cut and sewn into raw garments in Kentucky, and garment washed and finished in El Paso, Texas. I was sent on a three-week learning tour . . . no training manual, but hands-on experience with true craftspeople and seamsters. This was a time when garment manufacturing in the USA was a respected and desired industry. I was overwhelmed with respect for this talent and their commitment to excellence.

Over the next five years, I traveled around the world learning how to source and produce all kinds of garments for the Gap. In those pre-China-only manufacturing days, I spent time in Italy with our agent learning how merino yarn and sweaters were produced. This is when a new mentor entered my life, Maureen Skelly Bonini, who owned an Italian sourcing agency with her family. Gap Inc. was one of her largest clients, and eventually, partners. She was a fiery and adventurous Irish woman who had married an Italian man and raised four amazing children, while simultaneously running one of the most successful production agencies in Italy. Besides Gap Inc., the agency worked with legends like Ralph Lauren, Donna Karan, and Calvin Klein. She squired me all over Tuscany and Umbria, so I understood sweaters from the raw material stage . . . I actually saw the sheep before they were shorn and saw the raw wool before processing. I learned construction, costing, negotiation, and supply chain engineering. The education was amazing, and I am sad the young merchants of today do not get anywhere near that kind of hands-on experience or education. Our industry suffers from this lack of knowledge, and I see and feel it at many of the current offerings I find in stores.

Maureen also taught me about truly tasting and enjoying food, the glory of Italian red wines, limoncello after dinner, the proper way to eat Parmesan, how to make pasta like a native, and the cuisine and culture of Jamaica. She also introduced me to the merchants and events of the antique market in Paris, and how to respectfully negotiate and identify true quality and rare finds More than a business mentor, she became a sort of second Mama to me and one of the joys of my life was introducing my Mom and niece to Maureen in Paris in 2013. I cherish those memories and photos from that day. I thank her family for sharing her with me and allowing me to drink from her knowledge fountain. This was all part of my maturation as a merchant and a person. I was becoming a global citizen and developing my own taste and aesthetic. I was so lucky to learn from the best and the brightest.

Living in San Francisco during the 1980s and 1990s was also an education in managing and living with the public health crisis of AIDS. From some of the most passionate and driven people I had ever seen, I learned about activism, social justice, and infinite compassion. I volunteered on the AIDS Quilt, delivered food with Project Angel Food, and tried to raise money and awareness any way I could. As a gay man, you also learned about personal health and safety practices and were constantly submitted to testing and the agonizing wait for results. Safe sex was thrown in our faces and it was hard not to become bitter and frustrated about fairness and equity. Still, I would not trade that time for anything. I learned about community, authenticity, support, and love in all of its forms. My parents visited me a couple of times during this period, and it brought us closer as a family. I think it educated them as well, further proof about the value of lifelong learning and staying open. They even enjoyed a performance of the famous Beach Blanket Babylon and attended the Pride Parade. You can teach old dogs new tricks after all. Watching my parents belly laugh at the amazing cast of BBB was and is a treasured moment in my memory. I think it was a very important moment in forming an adult relationship and friendship with my parents.

The amazing pace of change in the retail and media industry is forcing me to learn and embrace new ideas regularly. My time at AwesomenessTV taught me about the power of the creator community and economy. I also learned the opportunities of short-form content and the pitfalls as well. I joined at the height of the Multi-Channel Networks (MCNs) craze and again was thrust into unfamiliar territory. Brian Robbins and Brett Bouttier were the founders and chiefs, and were very gracious to take time to work with me and my team in the nascent space of consumer products in this sector. It was another opportunity for personal growth and learning for me. As the former CEO of

Claire's retail company, I knew our business and marketing function were being disrupted by the trends in this space. I embraced a "disrupt or be disrupted" mentality and dove headfirst into the space. Teens and tweens were no longer trolling the malls to be with friends, they were doing it virtually and digitally through social media and YouTube, and I wanted to be part of this change. I am proud to say that we were the first MCN to embrace licensing and merchandising. We did a custom collection for Kohl's, had the first-ever booth for an MCN at the Licensing Expo, made the cover of *Licensing International* magazine, and had a holiday pop-up store on Fairfax Avenue in Los Angeles. My network and chosen family really kicked into full gear on that pop-up. Erin, Elizabeth, John, Lisa, Sharon, Danny, and more . . . people from all of my favorite teams were on this ride with me.

Believe me, we had so many more failures than successes, but the point was we were trying something new and learning from fact-based results. In addition, we had visionary leadership and supporters who allowed us to experiment and fail forward. Insights from these efforts completely influenced what we did with the global *Trolls* movie program at Dreamworks. Most of my AwesomenessTV team was absorbed into Dreamworks when I made the move to the Glendale team and campus, and they brought their openness and innovation with them.

You see, while I value lifelong learning personally for me, I also greatly admire that trait and energy in others. The human brain has infinite capacity and possibilities. Never edit your growth. Never stop asking questions and being open to new insights. By the way, I do not think being queer makes one any more or less inquisitive than our straight peers, but I do think it makes you keenly attuned to new information and active listening. I think queer people become very sensitive to verbal and visual cues in group situations, as we are constantly on guard for potential conflicts or judgment. My community is very good at "reading a room" and identifying potential problems. Sadly, this is a learned behavior and a necessary survival skill in many situations, but it is a tool nonetheless. Just another example of committing to lifelong learning and education.

I cannot stress enough the value of learning and growing throughout your career and life. How sad and boring to say, "I am done." It is why traditional retirement is not and was never a goal of mine. I encourage you to stay constantly curious and in the mode of eager sponge, soaking up what you can every day. Search new adventures and investigate how your skill set and experience can translate into new roles and even new industries. You must believe that anything is possible with some patience, perseverance, and confidence.

3 | Don't Let Anyone Dim Your Light

"My only regret about being Gay is that I repressed it for so long. I surrendered my Youth to the people I feared when I could have been out there loving someone. Don't make that mistake yourself. Life is too damn short."

— Armistead Maupin

I chose to start this chapter and my next learning based on this amazing quote by the brilliant creator of *Tales in the City*. Maupin perfectly summarizes my major personal regret as I review my life and that fear he references has impacted my professional career as well.

You see, although I suppressed my feelings and homosexuality in my youth, God had a different plan for me. I am effeminate, flamboyant, demonstrative, and have an odd and very female-sounding voice. In my entire childhood and high school experience I was horribly bullied. Physically, mentally, emotionally tortured on an almost daily basis. I was called every hateful name in the book. The fear and intensity of the situation was almost crippling. In the 1970s and early 1980s, no teacher or administrator in Toledo, Ohio, was trained or equipped to handle the situation. I did not report anyone. The fact is there was no one I trusted to report anything or discuss this situation. What was I going to say anyway? What they were calling me, no matter how cruel and harsh, was actually true. I did not deserve the bullying, but I struggled with rationalizing it. How twisted is that? I allowed myself to be bullied and harassed because I did not love myself enough to speak and own my truth. Nothing they said to me was worse than what I was saying to myself. In fact, I was internally bullying myself.

I was too smart for my own good. Instead of confronting the situation, I suffered in silence and misery, and except for some amazing friends (Amanda, Lori, Anne Marie, and my sister), no one even acknowledged what they witnessed. I had a group of tormentors at Whitmer High School (the Jocks) led by the star quarterback of the team who seemed to have a personal mission to terrorize and harass me regularly. I seemed to symbolize some kind of threat to them, and I was an easy target. I was punched, verbally abused, thrown into lockers, and generally hazed daily. At first, I would deny what they were saying. I would verbally fight back and tried to physically retaliate, but it never worked. I was always outnumbered. I would never cry, no matter how much it hurt, because I would not give them the satisfaction. It became a kind of morbid routine I reluctantly accepted. I started to hate going to school, which was so hard for me because I loved being in a good classroom. I came home with scrapes and bruises and lied to my parents about it happening in gym class, or having fallen or tripped. I think they knew what was really happening, but again, they were not equipped or ready to deal with the reality or have the tough conversations necessary to truly understand or address the situation. Bottom line, I did not feel safe at school. Adolescence, puberty, maturation are hard on everyone, but especially difficult for someone who is struggling with their sexuality and being harassed for their apparent or assumed differences. School is supposed to be a safe place to learn, grow, make mistakes, and prepare for life in the big world. It never felt that way to me. It felt like a harrowing obstacle course of self-loathing and seeking acceptance.

In hindsight, I am surprised I made it through that time. I was challenged daily and considered so many options to just make it all go away, including ending my life. It is hard to write that now, but I cannot write a book with an authenticity theme and not own how low and scared I felt as a teenager. Something kept me going. Some small flicker of confidence let me believe life was going to get better and easier at some point in the future. As a Midwesterner, I think I truly believed that what does not kill us makes us stronger, and that hard, honest work would bring positive change. This mental health struggle was a constant in my maturation. I am grateful that the topic of students' mental health and emotional well-being is discussed openly in many schools and settings today.

I am so grateful for teachers like Mrs. Elaine Kunz, who saw my struggles, but also saw my potential. I took my favorite classes with her, including American and British literature. I also did independent study with her and had some amazing, inspiring conversations about life, the world, and the future. One amazing assignment is when she asked me to write a paper about a contemporary piece of music and analyze the lyrics. I chose "Dust in the Wind" by Kansas. Haunting, prophetic, and insightful. I loved that song, still do, and loved that assignment as a 16-year-old. I was looking for a way out. I knew I had to get out of Toledo. I knew I had to change my environment and seek some kind of positive control.

I begged my parents to let me transfer to a smaller, private school, so I could avoid the daily suffering, but they were not supportive of that idea. As a member of student council, I participated in a day trip to Maumee Valley Country Day School and I saw kids who appeared to be "out" and happy. At least, I saw students who were "different" and also appeared to be struggling to be accepted. Until that visit, I did not think that was possible. As I said earlier, I became the "best" at anything else I could control (remember

Learning #1?). I knew I had to be better than anyone to get out of that situation, out of Toledo, to find people who accepted me. More urgently, I also had to accept myself and my story.

It got so bad, that my senior year in high school, after some of my older friends had graduated (my protectors), I asked my Mom to take me to an ear, nose, and throat specialist. I do not have a prominent, visible voice box, which is considered more female-like in appearance. I have a unique speech pattern and tone. I am consistently mistaken for a female on telephone calls, especially with customer service agents. To this day, I am often called "Mrs. Fielding" on phone calls. I love to make presentations and do public speaking engagements, but I hate to hear myself or see myself afterward. I can come across as very feminine in tone and speech pattern. I thought I needed surgery to change and deepen my voice. I learned that I also have shorter than normal vocal cords, whatever that means. I seriously considered having surgery to scrape and stretch my vocal cords in order to sound and appear more masculine or butch. I was convinced that if my voice was more masculine, I would be viewed differently and my life would be easier. I wanted to sound more like my Dad, who I thought of as very "male." I just wanted the tormenting and bullying to stop.

I think that was the most desperate moment of my teens. I considered what the world would be like without me. Even then, my parents were still not ready to have the "talk." Quite honestly, I was not ready to have the talk. I still did not understand myself, and I had no one to talk to honestly. We did however have some good conversations about accepting the way God made you. That was a slight door opening, but I was not prepared to walk through it yet.

In hindsight, I wonder what life would have been like if I could have accepted and embraced my truth at that point in my life. I doubt it would have been worse, but I mistakenly felt like I could play the game and hold out for something better. Again, I try to not live with regrets, but if I could, I would go back and try it as an out, proud teenager, rather than a closeted and bullied victim. I fantasized about somebody calling me fag, and I turned and say with a snap, "Damn right, honey!" I would have loved to attend school dances with a happy and handsome boy as my date. I would have enjoyed going to school in the morning without a constant state of dread and worry. I would have loved to develop self-confidence and self-appreciation at a much earlier age. I am constantly impressed by the young people I meet today who so easily embrace their truth and live the life they were meant to experience. I am grateful for their parents and schools that embrace their uniqueness with pride and provide open and supportive environments. I know it is never easy, but it gives me so much hope for the future.

In a sad, but interesting twist, I learned that my main high school tormentor/bully passed away at the age of 51 from CTE-type brain injuries from his football days. I learned this from my sister, who saw it on a Facebook post. Out of curiosity and a weird sense of closure, I decided to go on Facebook in January 2017 to read the story and what others had to say. What I saw and read there made me sick to my stomach and enraged me. I had an almost PTSD reaction to the postings. He was being eulo-gized as some amazing person who was taken too young from this earth and leaving behind a loving daughter and family. While I had sympathy for the family and agreed he was too young, I simply could not stomach making him into some kind of hero when he had hurt me so badly. I drafted a post on the wall three times, but never hit send to publish it. I wrote it, said it aloud, prayed for him, and then closed Facebook and have not been back on it since that moment. I never will go on it again. Old scars heal, but they are visible.

I am not proud of my reaction, and I had many therapist discussions about the experience but it taught me how much I still had to process from that period and what that bullying did to my psyche. "Progress, not perfection" is a great saying I learned in Al-Anon meetings, an incredible group I joined for the families and friends of people struggling with addiction. My shocking realization through a lot of work with therapists and friends is that I needed to forgive my bullies to move forward. That is still so hard to write and say aloud, but FORGIVENESS had to occur for my own sanity and peace of mind. I am not excusing their behavior or treatment of me, but hanging on to those horrible memories and scars was holding me back. I will never FORGET, but I do have the ability to FORGIVE.

I loved singing, dancing, and acting as a young child. Until 5th grade, I was very active in choir and theater classes and productions. I worked hard to get a solo and I enjoyed the spotlight very much. A highlight was my solo as Paul Revere in the musical *"Let George Do It."* I still remember all the words! In 5th grade, however, I started to learn that being in band, choir, or the arts was "gay" and certainly not for the cool kids. That label was already starting to haunt me, so I dropped out of anything that was remotely not perceived as straight, even though I found so much joy in those activities. That was the first time that I "dimmed my light." I was talented. I had a good voice. I was a natural showboat and I could make people laugh. My weakness and inability to handle the truth made me step out of something

I loved. My music teacher protested, but my parents did not say a thing. I think they actually understood why, even though we never discussed the decision in any meaningful way. We blamed it on my swim team practice schedule and other excuses, instead of the truth.

Today, I have a passionate love affair with live theater and experiences. I have seen over 200 plays and musicals all over the world. Asking me to rank my Top 10 musicals will take an entire evening of conversation. I also adore the art of drag. RuPaul's empire has solidified that love even more in the last few years. Thanks to the pandemic, I binge-watched the entire history of *Drag Race* in order. Choose me for your next trivia contest! To confess, I see myself up on that stage. I even have a drag name and persona developed, and when I am bored, I work on my run of show, my banter, and my choreography. I think there is a void in the market with the retirement of Dame Edna that I might just have to fill some day. I was devastated that the world lost dear Leslie Jordan in October 2022, as his personal story and presence were very inspirational to me. I still have his voice as my ring tone—"Well Shit, What Are Y'all Doing?"—will be with me forever. I know he had his struggles, too, but at the end of his life he was living fully out loud with joy.

I wonder often what my life would have been like if I followed my passion and talent. I wonder if I edited myself too severely and closed myself off to possibilities. I think that is why I cry like a baby when I see *Billy Elliott* or *Matilda the Musical*. Literally anything with children in key roles makes me weep with joy, mixed with a little regret. I allowed the bullies and societal norms and expectations to take away my gifts, drain my confidence, and ultimately, put my talents and passions in a box. I gave away power, and I have spent most of my adult life trying to take back the power.

I do believe I have fulfilled most of my destiny and have enjoyed the journey, but I cannot help but to wonder what it would have been like to try the entertainer role. I said I try to live without regrets and keep moving forward, but I truly regret not being strong enough to follow my passion and young talent. I am so blessed to have many friends in the entertainment industry now, and I work overtime to support their talent and endeavors because I am simply awed by their work. I think I was meant to be an enthusiastic fan, supporter, and producer . . . but I would love to go back and try that part of my life again. Never give away your power. Never dim your light.

I know that this is probably too much personal information and reflection, but I want to explain how this manifested in my professional life. This is Learning #3: Don't Let Anyone Dim Your Light.

My first professional story about my learnings in this area occurred in 2011. Since I was a bullied adolescent, I found myself to be a conflict-avoiding adult. Difficult and direct conversations were a weakness of mine that was called out in performance reviews. I had a tendency to apply the "Halo effect" to people, teams, and problems. This means that I actively searched for some redeeming quality in any person and would cling to that learning, rather than confront any performance or personality issues. I not only avoided conflict, I actively worked overtime to remedy any situation by taking most of the burden personally to find a solution. I became the ultimate caretaker, and that meant I was a popular team member and supervisor.

I also got assigned to many special projects. It also meant I could be easily manipulated and taken advantage of by people who saw my tendencies. This was the bullying memories manifesting in my professional life. I was simply trying to keep everyone happy, fly under the radar, and avoid confrontation.

For 10 years at Disney, I worked under the supportive leadership and direction of Andy Mooney. Andy was an energetic, intelligent, and visionary Scotsman who built a strong and diverse executive team for Disney Consumer Products. I was proud to work with such strong and intelligent peers, and we enjoyed many years of double-digit revenue and income growth as a team. Andy saw something in me he liked almost immediately when I joined the company in 2001. I was originally hired to run merchandising in the Disney Catalog, but after a corporate restructure I found myself in a similar role in Disney Store. That first stint in Disney Stores was very challenging, but Andy consistently checked in with me and asked me to hang in while he managed some important transitions. He trusted my confidentiality, and I trusted his word and vision.

In 2004, I was promoted to run the retail sales and marketing team globally. In late 2007, he asked me to step out of my role and work on a "secret project," and in 2008, I became the Disney Stores Worldwide President, as I referenced in the Learning #1 chapter. Andy was the perfect supervisor for me. He set ambitious goals, provided resources and support, and let me do my job. He always had my back, which in a large company like Disney, is so vitally important to any success. He believed in me, our team, and our vision for the Disney Stores. He never meddled, but he was always available when I needed his advice, support, or insights. I now see that he was asking me and enabling me to shine my light as bright as I could and he was there to be an ignitor.

Andy suddenly resigned from the company in fall 2011, while I was on vacation in Big Sur. I was shocked, confused, and angry, but I also felt oddly calm. I knew that Disney Consumer Products had a succession plan in place, and that I was on that list. I also knew the other names on that list, and I had enjoyed candid and open conversations with the other candidates. Due to the culture that Andy had created at DCP, the three of us agreed we would happily work for each other in any succession scenario. While I was sad and conflicted to see Andy depart, I felt like this may have been a new door opening for me.

I was asked to attend a group conference call, which I had to take from the resort manager's office as I had no signal or phone in my room. Picture this . . . it is 7:30 a.m. and I am sitting in some random office in a gorgeous resort in nature and my life changed in an instant. It was a group conference call of Andy's executive team, and I expected to hear that a search for a successor was underway and that it was business as usual. I also expected to hear from Andy on the reasons for his departure, but he was not on the call. My vanity allowed me to believe I was going to be contacted for an interview after they told us of his departure.

Imagine my surprise when Bob Chapek was announced as the new head of Disney Consumer Products. I think my heart actually skipped a beat. You could hear a pin drop on that call. I knew Bob, as he was the current head of Home Entertainment, and we had been in several meetings, work groups, and calls together. I was in shock. I had never considered Bob Chapek as a potential successor for DCP, and I expected an internal promotion from our own group. I expected, at least, a conversation or an interview personally. If not that, I expected one of my peers to be elevated to continue the good work and vision that was underway on the team.

As I was processing that initial news, we were then horrified to hear that DCP was perceived as weak, spoiled, and not team players by the rest of the company. We were told that Bob C. was brought in specifically to address our cultural and performance deficiencies. I was in a state of utter disbelief and confusion. I hung up and immediately reached out to Andy, who was not available. I corresponded with my work peers, and we were all similarly fumbling around with this rapid change of events. I returned to my room and spent the rest of that weekend and the end of my vacation in a kind of fog or haze.

When I returned to the office, the tension was palpable. I think the entire division was in disbelief. Nobody saw this coming. My office was in Pasadena, while the rest of the executives and teams were in Glendale, so that shielded us a bit from the upheaval, but you could feel the nervous energy everywhere. At the time of his departure, Andy's executive team had 10 experienced and diverse team members. We worked together and trusted each other, but almost immediately, you could feel the culture change. For the next few weeks, I attended the required executive team meetings and went about the business of Disney Stores.

Slowly, the dismantling of the prior regime began. I watched with disbelief as talented and strong professionals were suddenly dismissed from the team, seemingly for no reason except that they were "Andy's people." It was interesting to me that every time someone departed, they were replaced by someone from

Bob's prior division or team. It became obvious this change in leadership had been planned for some time.

I had an amazing EA (executive assistant), named Joanne Martino. She knew I was on edge, and I asked her to work the EA network to ascertain what was happening. The EA communication network at Disney was legendary, and you could count on that hotline for the inside truth. I asked her daily if I had been scheduled for a one-on-one meeting with my new boss. I was sure we had missed a call or an email as the weeks crept by and I watched more change occur. If you know the amazing Julia Louis Dreyfus show *Veep*, you know how I was with Joanne. I am referring to the scenes where the VP asks her assistant, Sue, if the president's office had called. Every day, I would ask if we had a call from Bob C.'s office. Every day, the answer was "no calls or emails."

Finally, after seven weeks of waiting, I was scheduled for a private meeting with Bob at his office. I studied and prepared for that meeting like it was my most important final in college, and the most important one-on-one in my career. I was three-and-a-half years into my tenure, and I felt positive about the changes and strategic plan progress, but I also was aware of our shortfalls. I thought we had built an excellent team and were exceeding customer expectations and had achieved a Disney level of service globally. The consumer and marketplace were moving more digital than physical, and I felt we had adapted to that fact as well. We also had strong financial performance and good return on investment metrics, so I thought we were OK both qualitatively and quantitatively.

I was not sure what to expect, and I had a nervous energy going into that meeting, although I did feel prepared for a professional update with my new boss. I understood the rocky history of the Stores at Disney, and was ready to be passionate, but not defensive and truly listen to his point of view and direction. As prepared as I was, I did not expect anything like what occurred that day.

There was no small talk or chit chat. Bob got right down to business and proceeded to tell me that he did not "like my business." When I pushed for details, I was offered vague mentions of working capital use, or ROIC metrics, and the consumer marketplace changing. I attempted to remain calm, but as I mentioned earlier, I do not have a great poker face, so I am sure my emotions surfaced and showed. He said he liked "licensing," as the IRR and other financial measures were more attractive. I felt like I was being bullied. It dredged up all my insecurities and lack of confidence. The meeting went horribly. I could not find any common ground with this man. We simply viewed Disney Store as if we were on two different planets. The final indignity was that I was informed I had to establish an office in Glendale, on the executive floor, to show I was a team player. Remember, my entire team was located 15–20 minutes (without LA traffic) away in Pasadena. Bob basically wanted me right outside his door.

I drove back to the Pasadena office in stunned silence. It felt as if everything was changing and that I had no options except to play the new game. I put on a brave face and attempted to keep it away from the Store's executives, but they could see what was happening. For almost five months, I played a game where I did not fully understand the rules and where the rules seemed to change daily. I watched 7 out of my 10 long-term, respected, and talented executive team peers leave. I was never sure if it was voluntary or involuntary, but I could see the trend and the truth. My Dad would have said he saw the handwriting on the wall. In fact, my Dad and I spoke more in that tumultuous period than in any other time in my career. It was hard for him, as he had never been in a similar situation, but he remained a constant source of reason and support. It became a routine to call him daily on my way home from work.

I felt somewhat protected, as I had two years left on a very nice contract, but the bullying and lack of respect for me and the business became very challenging. Being actively ignored and/ or challenged at every turn was a new sensation for me. I also felt like meetings and discussions about the Disney Stores were happening without my participation. I tried, in vain, to educate the new consumer product executives about the business and the importance of the Disney Store Experience to our overall Disney brand. Corporate Brand Management was an excellent partner for us in telling this story, but no facts seemed to work effectively on the new team. It became obvious I would be defending every strategic decision made since 2008, constantly, and the only KPIs (Key Performance Indicators) that mattered were financially based, ROI-focused, and what Bob C. decided was valuable. There was zero discussion about guest experience, or brand enhancement, or quality. I understood that I was going to be pushed to dismantle everything we had spent three-and-a-half years building.

I acknowledged and embraced the multiple challenges of running a primarily physical, global vertical retailer in a time of rapid movement to e-commerce, but our team was reacting and changing our business model. I started to doubt my abilities and everything we had done. I began to second guess all decisions. To be honest, my lifelong insecurities about my queerness was a hindrance in this situation. I allowed myself to believe I was "less than" the heterosexual leaders and in hindsight, that makes me so mad! I had worked so hard and was proud of what we had built and I was allowing uninformed bullies to tear down my confidence yet again, but this time it had ramifications beyond my own life.

I felt helpless and hopeless. For the first time in my career at Disney, I felt marginalized and diminished. The new culture and behavior were simply oppressive. I felt zero support. I would walk into a direct report meeting and not recognize the participants. At times, it felt like I was speaking another language. It was very hard to not personalize all the behavior and wear it on my face (no poker face, remember), but I owed it to my team to maintain a professional demeanor. Internally, I was a nervous and scattered leader with horrible self-talk in my head. I had never been "off the team" so dramatically at any stage in my career.

In a desperate attempt to regain my footing and protect the business and team, I threw a Hail Mary pass. I contacted the leader of another division within the company and asked for a coffee talk. This was someone I had worked with for 11 years and thought I had a confidential relationship with and could trust completely. I viewed him as a mentor and trusted his integrity and advice. I shared my story and concerns, and asked if he had ever considered moving Disney Stores into his business unit, as there were operational and guest experience synergies. He listened to me, promised to consider the suggestion, keep our conversation confidential, and get back to me. The minute I left his office, he must have picked up the phone or emailed my boss. Within days, I felt like I was dropped off in Siberia with a backpack and no map. While I truly felt this was a strategic move for the business unit, I guess I had come across as egocentric and self-serving. I had confirmed Bob's worst fears about me . . . I was not a team player and I was not on his program. I hope that young leaders understand this corporate politics example. For years, I had understood and thrived in the turbulent and difficult Disney corporate culture, and with one coffee meeting had triggered my inevitable departure. Please understand, my only regret is underestimating the situation and misreading my relationships so badly. I have a strong moral and ethical fiber and I will always fight for what I think is right, but I was ill-prepared for what happened next.

Whatever the perception, this was my new reality. I became a Harvard Business School case study of a disenfranchised and demotivated employee. I hit the realization that I was going to have to leave Disney. I was blessed with an amazing executive coach at Disney, named David Oldfield. I reached out to him to ask for an emergency session, and he patiently listened to my story and my emotions. He changed my life with one phrase, the one I am now sharing with you and the title of this Learning: "Do not let them dim your light." He made me realize that my boss and the company were asking me to change in a way I was uncomfortable with doing. I was being directed to lead and manage in a way for which I did not have the requisite passion or skill set. I was being asked to dim my passion and my natural abilities and personality. David also made me confront the reality that I could not change an entire division or the new culture or the way I was managed by Bob.

After that meeting, I felt lighter and more calm than I had in months, and I opened myself to the opportunities that the universe was bringing my way. I reached out to executive recruiters, letting them know I was open to new roles and to relocation out of state. Remember, I was under contract . . . I had to voluntarily resign; they really could not force me out. Within months, I had three CEO opportunities in retail. All of them were "fixer uppers," but with brands I respected. I felt it was time to make the leap to the next level and back to traditional vertical specialty retailing. I also felt like I had to take back control overall to some extent. It was not an easy decision.

I called the head of Consumer Products Human Resources and requested a meeting as soon as possible. I presented a formal letter of resignation and waited for her reaction. She was not surprised, and I could tell it was very hard for her as she had worked directly for me previously at the Stores and we had an excellent working relationship. She said she would share it with my boss and get back with me. I was confused, as I thought we would be planning the dates and transition scenarios immediately, but she simply said she would call me after discussing it with corporate. The next day, she called me and said I should take some time off while they formulated "the plan." I was shocked and bewildered. I had accepted a new job in Chicago that started in six weeks, and I wanted orderly closure at Disney before I made the move.

I spent the next two weeks at my home in Palm Springs, waiting for resolution and checking in regularly with HR. I was being dimmed, bullied, and managed, and realized I was not in control at all. I was lying to everyone, except my wonderful executive assistant Joanne. She was the only one who knew the truth. I hated every minute of it . . . it was torture and it dredged up so much old baggage.

Finally, I received a call on Memorial Day weekend with the exit package and the news that the following Tuesday (the day after the holiday) was to be my last day at Disney. I was to report to work very early to clean out my personal belongings and be out of the office before most employees would arrive for their normal workday. No time to meet the team. No time to say goodbye. No closure. The Mouse House had spoken and was in charge, and if I failed to agree and execute their instructions, I would jeopardize my exit agreement, my stock options, and my pension. I was in shock. I had given almost 12 years of my life to this company and was willing to do a professional and orderly exit and transition. Selfishly, I wanted to spend time with my team to thank them properly and say goodbye. I wanted them to understand how grateful I was for their hard work and support. And, finally, I wanted to control the rumors and the narrative. I did not trust anyone at Disney to tell the proper story after what I had witnessed for the last year.

I called Joanne and she agreed to meet me at the office at 6:30 a.m. on that Tuesday with plastic tubs to get my personal items packed and out to my car. She was, always, a rock and a calming professional.

Tuesday came and Joanne and I worked as fast as we could to grab what I needed and wanted. Our offices were all glass, so it was very obvious what was happening. Around 8 a.m., the early birds started to arrive, and you could start to feel a sense of dread and odd buzz in the office. I had been spotted and it was pretty clear what was transpiring. Around 8:45, I looked at Joanne and said I had to get out of there, and she could get the rest of my stuff later.

As I walked down the stairs carrying my final tub, I realized there was a group of people in the lobby kitchen break area. I could not avoid passing them, so I tried to hurry through when a round of applause broke out. I started sobbing. There were coffee and bagels and donuts and people in a big circle. A wonderful former team member, John, had arranged everything that morning. I was overcome with gratitude and sorrow simultaneously. There were tears, laughs, and goodbyes. There was also a lot of confusion and frustration spilling out. I am eternally grateful for those precious 30 minutes. No one knew where I was going, they just knew I was moving on. Most importantly to me, they knew I made the decision. There would be many subsequent rumors that I was forced out, but for that one moment, I had taken control back from the bullies. I was going to shine my light. Our motto and guiding vision at Disney Store was "The best 30 minutes of a family's day," and my team gave me that on my way out the door completely.

An interesting side note. The next day, I had a goodbye coffee meeting with Bob Iger, the CEO of Disney. In that meeting, I told him I was going to be the CEO of Claire's Stores, Inc. and would be moving to Chicago. He was so kind and gracious and offered me excellent advice about what being a CEO meant and lessons he had learned. What did Bob tell me that day? I will never forget his guidance and wisdom. First, he said that my job as CEO was to be an excellent communicator, set a strategic vision, hire great people, and get out of their way. He also talked to me about board management and inventor relations, as I had not really had that experience to date. Finally, he talked to me about managing creativity. I did not have a notebook with me, but I ran back to my car and scribbled down these tips. I had heard him speak on this topic several times, but these five tips were the most insightful and concise, and perfectly illustrate his leadership philosophy.

Tip 1: Don't take a hierarchical approach.
Tip 2: Don't create an approval process that is unduly rigorous.
Tip 3: Be careful not to water down ideas or lose people's passion.
Tip 4: Let those in charge make decisions.
Tip 5: Put the spotlight on the company, not the individual.

I have used his guidance and wisdom ever since that day in all of my work.

Fast forward to November 20, 2022. My phone starts lighting up with texts and group chats and my news feed is firing on all cylinders. Bob Iger is coming back as Disney CEO and Bob Chapek is done. I had been gone from Disney for over 10 years, and still, this news has taken me right back to my departure and my reasons for leaving. There is a certain satisfaction in reading this news and all the reactions from current and former cast members. Most are overjoyed and you feel optimism from the team that has been missing for the last few years.

Bob Iger is an amazing leader, especially in times that require communication and change management, so the decision makes sense. The abruptness of the board decision, especially after recently renewing Bob Chapek's contract, is a bit of a headscratcher, but I guess they wanted immediate action and impact. I wish the Disney team much luck and success as they manage this transition.

I am confident that the creative community will be managed more effectively and with more skill now. I will be cheering for its collective success and watching, listening, and learning. What struck me most was Bob Iger's initial comments about returning to elevating creativity and storytelling and eliminating hierarchy. He was returning to his natural style and adapting it to the present realities of the marketplace and the company performance. So much to watch and learn.

I also could not help but reflect on my own exit and how I had no true closure with my direct boss. In a weird way, I will not lie, I thought . . . well, karma is a bitch. While I had that excellent exit opportunity with Bob Iger, I never had an exit interview from human resources. I never heard from my boss. I have not spoken to him since I left the company. Almost 12 years at Disney was over. The final straw was that two of my senior management team leaders were promoted to replace me. These were people I had recruited, rewarded, traveled the world with, and thought I knew personally. I worked directly with them for four years and felt a bond of trust and mutual respect. I learned that day that they had been actively working against me with Bob C. and had been lobbying for this role for months. In hindsight, I realize other people saw their behavior and tried to warn me, but I had a blind spot. I was vulnerable and trusting, and they used that against me. That was a painful moment and lesson. It did not feel like the most "Magical Place on Earth" at the end, but I left with pride and amazing memories. It was time to shine my light somewhere else.

Being president of Disney Store was the best role I have ever held and it was taken away from me based on factors I never understood or could control. It was more than a job to me; it was a passion. I am not stupid; I know it is a big corporation and that there were forces working to undermine me, but

I never thought my tenure would end with me carrying plastic tubs full of memories away with tears streaming down my face. It was a gut punch and while time has dulled the pain and I have new stories to share, I will never be fully over the end of that chapter.

Still, in my continuous drive for personal growth, closure, and moving forward, I realized recently that I need to forgive Bob C. and the entire Disney hierarchy for that episode and my departure. I saw myself retiring from Disney after making magic for many more years. To this day, I do not fully comprehend why things transpired the way they did, I may never fully understand. When the vision of my future was not possible, it brought out the worst in me and others. So, I needed to forgive to be able to focus on all the wonderful, positive memories and moments from my 12 years there. Again, FORGIVE, but not FORGET. My Disney chapter is the most important element of my life story to date. I had to learn, I had to grow, and I had to leave to continue my authentic journey.

★ ★ ★

I was announced as the CEO of Claire's Stores and began in June 2012, hired by the famous PE (private equity) firm that had performed a LBO (leveraged buyout) a few years prior. I was the second CEO, which should have served as a cautionary warning sign for me, but I plunged ahead anyway. I kept telling myself that I was not running away from Disney, but that I was running to the opportunity to be a retail CEO. The PE firm actively courted me for months and said all the right things in the interview process. The company wanted me to reinvigorate Claire's the way we had reinvented Disney Store. I had not heard wonderful things about the PE firm, but I was confident, or arrogant, enough to think I could be successful.

Please note, I am including this life lesson in the "Don't Let Anyone Dim Your Light" chapter of the book for a reason. I had always worked for large corporations and was not exposed to the intricacies of private equity, investor relations, board govern-ance and management, or managing a large amount of institu-tional debt. I was unprepared for the realities of being a CEO in a highly leveraged company, owned by a PE firm that only wanted a return on their investment. I should have pushed harder to speak to CEOs of other companies the PE firm was invested in or had run. I should have done more research and homework. I thought I was prepared and smart, but this chapter of my career was humbling. I hope people learn from my expe-rience as they consider their own career choices.

I dove in with all my strength, enthusiasm, and experience I could muster. I read all the books about becoming a CEO. I joined local CEO organizations to network and learn from others. I built my executive team, including bringing important people from my past who shared my vision for experiential retail and e-commerce at Claire's. I bonded with the existing executives and quickly grew an important relationship with the CFO, whom I grew to trust completely and rely on throughout my tenure. My truth teller, Peter, came to Chicago to be in the C-suite as the chief people officer. I felt like we had a good team in place.

There were, however, strategic disconnects with the PE firm almost immediately. The board of directors, all appointed by the PE firm and loyal to them, were all straight, white, older men.

I pushed to diversify the board with female directors, or people from marketing and e-commerce, with no success. It made no sense to me that a brand focused on tween and teen females did not have a female voice in the room. We had no true representation of our community or target customers in the boardroom.

In the first year, we were making some progress and I was slowly getting my footing. The board was somewhat supportive of the mission and vision I had for the business. I had inherited a broken business with a massive amount of leveraged debt, and I needed to work fast and take risks to correct the trajectory. I traveled around the world to meet employees and partners on their home turf. I was very conscious of presenting a positive and can-do attitude to our global teams and vendors, and I was very aware of managing my queerness in certain countries and cultures. That was not easy for me after years of preaching authenticity, but I had to do what was right for the success of Claire's. I don't think I had ever worked harder in my life. I know I had never traveled that much in my career. It took a toll on my physical health, my mental health, and on my relationship. My partner had moved with me to Chicago, and I basically was never there to provide the normal amount of support he deserved, let alone anything extra.

My insecurities as a first-time and queer CEO plagued me endlessly. I was constantly second guessing myself and spent many sleepless nights considering strategic options for the business. The PE firm's management style was tough for me. It was very data- and numbers-driven, and I felt they had unrealistic expectations. They were very direct and harsh, almost bullying and did not really listen to what I or my team was telling them. I would get regular short phone calls and a few in-person meetings where they were quick to point out the issues but offered relatively few action suggestions or innovative ideas. I just kept doubling my efforts to turn around the business trend and win their support. It was a very challenging situation, but I felt compelled to meet and exceed what they were asking from the team. My insecurities were a hindrance. I own the fact that my lifelong feelings of being "less than" really were a burden and hurt my performance. That is really tough to write and admit, as I am a proud man.

I wish I had admitted my needs and shared my vulnerabilities with someone. The reality was that I was a bit of a unicorn as an out, queer CEO. I did not have a natural network or many peers. I had allies and found myself reaching out to my female CEO friends for guidance and insight, as I did not feel much kinship with other CEOs at that time. The reality is I was not confident enough to ask for the guidance or the listening ear I needed.

To be honest, it felt like I was working overtime for their approval and was very reminiscent of previous experiences in my life, particularly with male authority figures. I am extremely coachable if I feel listened to and supported. I believe in listening to the wisdom and guidance of experts and trusted leaders. I operate with a "two heads are better than one" style. The issue here was I did not think they were speaking with any real insights into the business, the consumer, or the marketplace. In contrast, when I am ignored or bullied, I fight back and get defensive. Those situations do not bring out the best in me. I am like an animal backed into a corner. My emotions come to the surface, and I can appear weak and indecisive. I hate feeling like that.

The power dynamic with the board felt very stacked against me and the executive team. They were very difficult to present anything to, and I had to manage many ruffled feathers and hurt feelings on my team after one of our sessions. As I write this in 2022, it is interesting to note that Claire's went through a bankruptcy filing and is under new investors, leadership, and ownership. Their current strategy has underpinnings of what our team developed in 2013 and 2014, including their shops in Walmart and drug stores. That gives me a little internal smile and a little confidence shot. I wish the current team nothing but success. I do love that brand and those customers.

In October 2012, my Dad was diagnosed with stage 4 pancreatic cancer and given a three- to six-month timeline to live. My parents lived in Phoenix, Arizona, and I was four months into my CEO tenure, living in Chicago. I immediately flew to them to have family time and get his affairs and wishes in order. The board was initially supportive, and I was working from my parents' house as we dealt with the myriad of emotions and tasks that accompany a terminal diagnosis. Imagine being a first-time retail CEO going into the holidays with the impending loss of your father. I was on autopilot and compartmentalized as much as I could. I knew we had to focus as a family on my Dad's wellness and needs, and to clarify insurance, social security, and benefits for Mom. I spent three weeks in Phoenix in October, and left feeling accomplished and sad, and grateful that we had that time together.

My Dad was a candidate for the Whipple procedure to potentially remove his tumor, and that was scheduled for November 19. I returned to Phoenix to be with him and the family for the surgery feeling somewhat optimistic and focused on staying positive. As a retail CEO, I was staying focused on the preparation for Thanksgiving and Black Friday, and was working 12 hours a day in between the family time, memories, and games to keep our minds off of the surgery. None of us slept the night before the surgery, and we needed to have him at the hospital by 6 a.m. Three hours into the surgery, his surgeon emerged to inform us that the surgery was not going to work, so they were sewing him up and sending him to recovery. His oncologist told us that with chemotherapy and radiation, he may have three to six months to live.

My Mom and sister were catatonic. I was numb. Suddenly, we realized that one of us would have to tell him the news when he woke up and we could see him in the recovery room. I was nominated, and when I turned the corner of his space, my Dad looked at me and said "It is not good news, is it?" I immediately began to cry and asked him how he knew, assuming his doctor or a nurse had beat me to it. Dad pointed at the clock in the recovery room and noted the time. He knew he was supposed to be in surgery for six to eight hours, and it was only four hours since he had gone in. . . . I will never forget thinking, "Of course, my attention-to-detail Dad would notice that!" Dad stayed in the hospital for almost 10 days recovering from the surgery. I visited him on November 29, on my way to the airport to return to Chicago, and hugged him and said I would see him at Christmas. He knew it was time for me to get home to my job in Chicago.

My father passed away while I was in the air to O'Hare airport. I landed to dozens of texts and calls from my sister, and I collapsed in baggage claim. My partner gathered me and our luggage and got me home. By this time, I had spoken to my sister and my Mom, and I got a flight for early the next morning to return to Phoenix. On that day in November 2012, I felt like an adult for the first time in my life, and I did not like that feeling at all. I was now the man in the family. I had to be the ultimate caretaker and organizer. I know everyone goes through this natural life event, but nothing prepared me for the grief I felt when I lost my Dad.

And yet, there is a business story in all of this and a critical learning I need to share with all of you. The morning after my Dad's passing, prior to getting on a plane to organize his funeral and last wishes, I needed to do an analyst earnings call for Claire's. Per Brodin, our excellent CFO, had it all written and ready. I did not practice. I simply drove to the office, sat in the room with him and others, and delivered the script. I did not take questions. I could not take questions. I was on zero sleep, running completely on adrenaline. I do not remember anything else about that call, except for a driver taking me to the airport directly after it for my flight to Phoenix.

That month of December 2012 is a blur of work/family/funeral/sleepless nights. I attempted to make Christmas 2012 special as we were all in mourning. I became Martha Stewart, Ina Garten, and Queer Eye for the Straight Guy combined and went so overboard on decor that it was borderline embarrassing. We had lights and trees and yarn decor everywhere. I wanted my family to have a good holiday, even though we were all still grieving. The food from friends and colleagues never stopped coming in and we ate away our pain.

I do remember vividly being on the phone at 7 p.m. with my board on Christmas Eve while my family sat at the dining table waiting for me. The board wanted to discuss the terms of an endorsement deal we were negotiating, and I was not strong or secure enough to tell them they were out of line. I was still so new and I was passionately committed to the deal in question, so I spent 45 minutes trying to get their approval to proceed. When I returned to the dinner table, I could not handle the look of disappointment and disapproval in my family's eyes. The next day, Christmas, I knew I had made a mistake in my choice of job. While I felt my vision and talent was appropriate for Claire's, it became obvious that the numerous conflicts with the board were making the situation untenable.

I had never felt this sense of failure in my career. My light was not only being dimmed, it was being fully extinguished. I had made a bad decision and had passed on other opportunities that might have had more success. Maybe I was running away from Disney more than I had previously acknowledged, but something was very wrong. Even though I was in the throes of grief, I spent that break figuring out how to fix the situation with Claire's and what a Plan B would look like if I could not make it happen.

I loved the Claire's people, brand, and the opportunity, but I had failed to ask the right questions and research the PE firm more deeply. I learned that I like to lead creative functions and guest experience roles, and that my lifelong goal of being a CEO was disappointing and I lacked the necessary passion for that situation. The role was actually dimming my light.

As CEO of a PE-backed firm, you are constantly managing your board, your investors, and your P&L statement. In this case, I also needed to manage the leveraged debt and interest payments. I love working on product, store design, service and team development. None of those skills were recognized or rewarded in this CEO role. I had been warned about the loneliness of the CEO role, that everyone in the company works for you, so you have no peer network. I built an amazing team of executives and I networked with other CEOs in the Chicago area, looking for some kind of formula or insight. I had moved my partner and our dogs across the country, away from family and friends. The stress and self-doubt were overwhelming. In addition, I was dealing with the grief of losing my father.

Still, I had a job to perform and I had made commitments to many people, so I doubled down on my work and tried to solve this puzzle. In the middle of my tenure, I had an executive physical. As part of that work, I met with a psychiatrist who specialized in executive performance. During our sessions, he helped me realize I was not properly processing my grief or managing my personal needs. The gift I received from losing my father the way I did was newfound perspective. His loss taught me that life was too short and that it was not worth sacrificing your health or wellness for anything. It took me another 15 months to muster the strength to resign that CEO role. In April 2014, I resigned and worked until June. I had made it two years in the most challenging role of my career, but I was ready to find something better and more suited to my strengths and talents. I left older, wiser, and more cognizant of what overall health meant to me. I called a few select friends and mentors and told them I was "available."

My final thought and piece of advice in this chapter is about helping others shine their lights. Once you understand the concept of not ever dimming your own light, or letting others dim it for you, I believe you must commit to helping others grow and learn the skill.

A woman named Francesca, who worked for me at Disney in Italy, was always one of my favorite team members. She was smart, energetic, educated, passionate, and radiated positive energy. She taught me the concept of being a "pearl hunter." At one of our group meetings in Europe, I asked her to share her story and this piece of wisdom. Essentially, she encouraged hiring managers and other leaders to look for pearls. She felt everyone had skills and traits that made them unique and special, just like finding a pearl in an oyster. It was our job as leaders to create opportunities and projects that allowed the pearl to be cultivated and shined. When pearls are first found, they are rough, dull, and dirty. With the skilled hand of a jeweler, they become beautiful with a soft glow that dances in the light. Francesca educated us that true leadership and people management and development was a similar process. To build effective teams, you needed to be a pearl hunter.

That really stuck with me, and I reference that learning often in my work. I think it is an excellent illustration of helping someone find and shine their light, and never asking them to dim it for anyone or any role. My most important learning to share is NEVER dim your own light, and find other people and diverse opportunities that allow your light and energy to burn brighter. People in your life need to ignite and enhance your light . . . and be ready to bask in the warmth and glow. You are blessed with natural and learned talents and earned knowledge. Shine that light and share it with the world.

4

Find and Embrace All Your Families, Especially the Ones You Choose

We are all born into some kind of family structure, and all have relative degrees of functionality, success, and challenges. No family is perfect, despite all outward appearances and social media posts. I am a firm believer in the effects of birth order, and in both nature and nurture helping to form us as human beings. I have seen all kinds of family-type units around the world, and I am convinced that finding your chosen family is one of the keys to stability and happiness in your life. I also think your chosen family has more impact on your professional life than your natural family in many ways.

For many marginalized groups, their only choice for support and community is to build or find a chosen family. There are too many examples of people in our community who have been disowned by their family when they embrace their story. Embracing their authenticity may cause immense ruptures with their parents, siblings, and extended relatives. The chosen family steps in to give safety, understanding, and unconditional love. I am sure many people have naturally formed these circles of support without putting a name like "chosen family" on the group. Many people may not even consciously search out this level of friendship and support, but I feel it is vital, especially in this challenging world.

Building and finding your community, your tribe, your trust circle, your BFFs is different for everyone, but you know who the members of your group are instinctively. These are the people who truly define unconditional acceptance and love. This does not mean they do not challenge you, or push you, or sometimes just piss you off. The key is that they are your truth tellers. Your ride or die posse. These are the people whom you can not talk to for three years and pick right up naturally when you reconnect. You share a history. You share experiences. You sometimes share common beliefs and opinions, but not always. Regardless, they keep you humble. They remind you of your roots and your foundation and your history. They are a great ego check and/or ego booster, depending on the circumstances. They connect you to your past, present, and dream your future with you. Chosen families provide an essential kind of love and support that sometimes your natural family does not have the ability to provide.

I have been so fortunate to have strong groups of friends from various points in my life. My Indiana University tribe is so unique and special. Imagine meeting your best friends on day one of college at 18 and still being close 40 odd years later. This tribe is truly my "ride or die." They love me as simply "Jim" and have been with me at every pivotal moment of my life. Our group has been through marriages, births, divorce (only mine!), and deaths of family and parents. We also lost one of our group very early to cancer, and I think that made us recommit to the importance of our tribal memories, gatherings, and customs. These are the people who hold all of my secrets and stories. As a queer man, they have provided me with unbelievable gifts . . . as each of them have brought a new generation into our community. There is something so rare and unique about spending time with the children of your best friends. Watching them grow and mature and enter adulthood, bringing little pieces of their parents and our shared stories with them. I am so supremely grateful to have this access and special time with all of them.

This book is not an autobiography, but I cannot write this chapter without acknowledging Linda, Lisa, Leslie, Mark, Mary, Bill L., and Bill N. They know how much I love them. They know how much I need them. I do not think they realize how much they shaped me and guided me, and how I owe so much of my successful journey to their friendship. I hope reading this book will help them understand how grateful I am for their love and support.

My overseas study experience in Copenhagen, Denmark, is another wonderful example of forming a family. I chose to live with a Danish family and was very lucky to be in a home with an 18-year-old Danish sister and 21-year-old Danish brother, Anna and Soren. The Christensen family embraced me from day one and always spoke Danish to me, which made me conversationally fluent in six months. I even got to spend time with the grandparents! I actually turned 21 in Copenhagen, and the Christensen family made it so special and unique. The program I was in brought together students from Australia, Canada, and all over the USA. I met amazing people from everywhere, and we formed a life-long bond of shared experiences. To this day, I am still in touch with many of them, and see my friend, John M., often. We reconnected at an Apollo investment event in Beverly Hills, never expecting to run into each other like that. It goes to show that your found and chosen families can pop up anywhere, so take time to cherish and nurture them.

Luckily, I am blessed with an incredible natural or birth family. Yes, I did have and still have many challenges with my parents. My Dad did not understand how much I needed him to nurture our relationship more. I have already talked about the challenges with my Mom and her disease. Today, we are dealing with aging and dementia, and the inevitable role reversal that happens as our parents hit their later lives. It is also important to celebrate the many amazing stories and memories that we have as a family, especially with Dad gone and Mom's diagnosis. I feel like I needed to share my truth and the darker side of our history, but I also have so many happy stories about the special times we

spent as the 4 J's. My Dad would save all of his vacation and personal days, and we would embark on three- to four-week boat
trips around the Great Lakes. My parents never missed a swim
meet and volunteered as judges, timers, and hospitality tent cap-
tains. They were present for every school function. We laughed
A LOT. My entire family has a wicked sense of humor, and we
could just look at each other in silly ways and burst out laughing.
My Dad loved to drive, and we were the Road Trip family, with
similar adventures to the Griswolds in *National Lampoon's Vacation*
movie series. My Dad was retired military, so we learned how to
void on demand and on his schedule because nothing was going
to stop him from breaking his time record from Toledo to
Ft. Lauderdale at the holidays. I know no family is perfect, but I
do feel blessed, and now understand that all of the good times and
bad times are necessary to grow and learn. I realize now that I am
a perfect combination of my parents in every way, and that their
union and efforts are the core of what I bring to the world daily.

My sister is an eternal blessing, friend, and confidante. She was
my first best friend. Jill and I have been at this for more years
than we care to admit, but I cannot imagine a better little sister.
I am constantly in awe of her ability to build a successful career,
marriage, and family. I love when she calls me and says "Hi, Big
Brother." My sister has managed rheumatoid arthritis for almost
20 years now, since the birth of her second daughter. My Dad's
nickname for her was "Rocky," and when she was diagnosed, he
always used to share this little story. He would say that God
knew Jill would handle and manage the situation with strength,
true grit, and grace. He then would add that if the situation was
reversed and I had that diagnosis, I would be curled in a ball and
in the ICU of the closest hospital. He always said that Jill would
fall in a pile of poop and come out smelling like a rose, while

I tended to fall deeper into the pile. Any wonder who his favorite was? It always made us laugh and still makes me smile.

Honestly, Jill has the best qualities of our parents. She is whip smart, truly funny, compassionate, charming, and passionately committed to her family. She also has calm and gratitude traits that somehow were not present in my time in the womb. Sometimes I wonder how we have the same lineage! She calls me on my BS constantly. She knows my moods and triggers better than anyone, and can pull them at will. She has maintained solid friendships since elementary school and started building her chosen family at a very early age. Wisdom, grace, beauty . . . I wish everyone had a Jill as their sister. By the way, we fought mean as kids, especially with the verbal jabs. We can make each other cry at the drop of a hat!

When I came out to her, a full four years before I told my parents, it was a bit of a small disaster. . . . I think it was a true test of our sibling relationship. She did not handle it well, and we both realized with hindsight that she was too young, naïve, and gullible to hear my truth. She had been too sheltered, and I think she had all types of terrible stereotypes in her mind. The same ones I had been raised with and filled my self-talk. She told me that I had always been her hero and she kept me on a pedestal, and this was the first thing that knocked me off that perch. It was awkward for six months after I told her. Everything felt off in our normally easy communication and relationship. We worked through it by her asking questions that made us both uncomfortable, and me managing my expectations and letting her learn and grow. At one point, seemingly without reason or cause, she was back to being my Rocky and we moved forward. I realize now that she was also protecting me. Her reaction was about her fear of how I would be treated in the world and potentially hurt by people. She could not articulate it then, but we both fully understand that perception and reaction now.

Since that initial rough period, she has never wavered in her unconditional love and support and I cherish our times together. In fact, I love our times together so much that I am actually happy my nieces are grown and I get to spend alone time with Jill again. I know that is incredibly selfish, but it is how I feel. Nothing like a healthy and honest interaction with your sibling. My sister, with her strength and wisdom, was the glue in our family, especially during my coming out process. She was a bridge builder and loyal friend, and always made me feel safe and loved.

My final natural family story is about my brother-in-law Brian and the arrival of my beautiful nieces, Katherine and Samantha. I hit the jackpot with Brian. Jill used my story and orientation as a type of litmus test for anyone she dated. Jill and I lived in Chicago together early in both of our careers, and it was an amazing period of our relationship to be adults together out on our own. As I was leaving for San Francisco, she told me she had met a special guy named Brian at a friend's Thanksgiving Day dinner. She told me all about him, but I remember the most important fact about this man. He played on a gay softball team in a mixed league, simply because he liked the other people on the team. BONUS POINTS × 10! The rest is history and I received so many amazing gifts with his inclusion in our family. When Katherine and Samantha (Katie and Sammie) arrived in this world, I felt a form of love I had not known before. One of the hardest things about being gay in the 1980s and 1990s was that you felt you were giving up any hope for children. With the arrival of legal adoption and surrogacy, today is a different story. For my generation, however, children were very rare, unless someone had them from a prior heterosexual relationship. The first time I held Katie and Sammie, it closed a small hole in my heart and my parental urges and needs were quenched. I immediately understood what role I was meant to play in their lives. Spending time with them, watching them grow, and feeling their impact on the world is one of the joys of my life.

I felt somehow more complete and I felt a radiating love and protective instinct. I soon learned that being a gay uncle or "guncle" was a perfect role for me and a true gift from the universe. You get to spoil and love on them, and then you get to send them home. My nieces were at the perfect ages along my career path. They benefited from the complete Disney experience, including role-play sets, park visits, cruises, and character meet-and-greets. When I was CEO of Claire's, they loved the swag boxes and VIP meet-and-greet with Katy Perry, who was lovely to my entire family. I always called Katie my Disney niece, as it was easy to track her age with my tenure at the company. My sister and brother-in-law gave me the ultimate gift, they made me an uncle. People get tired of hearing me brag about Katie and Sammie, but they are true lights in my life.

My chosen family, in the meantime, made me a godfather to three amazing young people in addition to Katie. I am proud to touch each of their lives and I hope I add a small amount of value and wisdom along their path. I have watched Sara and Roman grow into exceptional young people who are going to make massive differences in our world, each in their own way. My latest goddaughter, Lola, is the glorious daughter of Jay and Olivia, whom I met in 2016. They amazed me by asking me to perform their marriage ceremony as well. It was my first time in that role, and it was one of the honors of my life. There is always room for special additions to your chosen family, new branches for your tree, and stories for your memory books and journals.

* * *

So how does this learning relate to the business world and my leadership journey?

My advice is relatively simple and not that unique, but it is never easy.

Be a team builder, leader, and player. Learn when to lead, when to follow, and when to change course. When I am building a team or hiring for a position, I am constantly evaluating the rest of my team's skills and needs to determine if this candidate will be a fit. I build and value high-performance cultures, and I want everyone to feel they are valued and making a contribution. In the previous chapter, I wrote about being a "pearl hunter." That skill helps you build engaged, energetic, and diverse teams. I also look for "helicopter ability" in my executive-level direct reports. This means I value people who can not only hover and be strategic and visionary, but also have the skill to swoop down to the ground and be tactical and operational when necessary. The key is how long it takes them to lift off the ground again and get back up to strategic hovering. You can and should test for this ability in interviews. Ask open-ended questions that look for this critical skill. And, remember to build teams of complementary skills and diverse backgrounds. You do not need a bunch of clones or competitors. If you are good at your role, you can lead many types of people with success. The simple joys of a team performing at its best are some of the best memories of my career.

I also encourage you to search for mentors, and to be a mentor. I am at this point in my life because people saw something in me and gave me opportunities to stretch, learn, and grow. They allowed me time to learn from mistakes and study issues and try a variety of solutions. I worry sometimes that we expect too much of our young talent and that our success-oriented culture does not allow for organic growth and maturation. I think it is critical to experience many different types of roles and jobs early in our careers, so we do not get pigeonholed or tracked too early. If someone has a passion for something early, of course, I say go for it . . . that is living authentically. There is tangible value, however, in allowing a career to naturally develop. I also had a group of senior queer leaders in my industries who reached out to help me navigate the shark-infested waters that could appear at times. Mentorship is a serious two-way commitment, so do not enter a relationship quickly or lightly. Make sure you have time to be there for your mentee or mentees, and that you establish trust and confidentiality early in your partnership. In a complex and challenging society and marketplace, mentorship relationships are vitally important to success.

One of my earliest realizations about a work chosen family member was my partnership with Elliot Staples at the Gap. When I was named the men's sweater associate merchandise manager, Elliot was the head designer for sweaters and knits, based in New York City. Elliot was a very successful designer, a knit product development expert, and one of the leaders of NYPD (New York Product Development) at Gap. In those heady days at Gap, you and your business performance were heavily influenced by your relationship with your NYPD partner. Mickey Drexler encouraged the yin and yang of the San Francisco office/New York office perspectives and felt that true creativity was born out of that creative tension and geographic differences.

I won the designer lottery with Elliot. He taught me so much and stretched me to take risks and move beyond the traditional tennis V-neck sweater that was a basic at Gap. We traveled the world together working on inspiration, sourcing, and price negotiation. Over time, we developed an easy and collaborative work style, and became adept at almost reading each other's thoughts. We also kept our healthy creative tension and had some heated arguments, but our line was always better because of those moments. Elliot was the first "creative" I worked with, and he taught me so much about artistic sensibility and talent. We began working together in 1994. We both went our separate ways after Gap, but we have never failed to stay in touch, and we are always there for each other professionally and personally. In an odd twist, I was on the Board of Advisors for the Limited for about 18 months, and Elliot was the lead designer for the brand. Full circle moment. Never underestimate true connection.

Another great story about chosen family or work family is my stint at Fox as head of Consumer Products and Experiences. I was very hesitant to accept this role initially. I knew the previous leadership team and had tremendous respect for its members, but I knew their jobs had been very challenging and that the culture at Fox Consumer Products had a bad reputation in our industry. What made me think I could be successful in the same role?

I agreed to a lunch meeting with the incredible Stacey Snider, the chairman of the movie studio. I hoped to secure a six-month consulting role to kick off my newly formed agency, which I had named Intersected Stories. As this lunch progressed,

I became more impressed with Stacey's energy and vision for the role, and she confirmed to me that I would also have responsibility for the television side of the business, including FX Networks, which I found very intriguing. I agreed to meet with Peter Rice, Dana Walden, Gary Newman, and John Landgraf. With each meeting, I became more interested and excited. These people were so smart and so experienced and were creating great stories, so I wondered, "Why couldn't I make this work?" I respected the history and the library of Fox and was ready for a new challenge.

I learned that due to a series of voluntary resignations and involuntary terminations, there were over 35 openings on the organization chart for this group. This included, literally, the entire senior leadership team. If I took on this challenge, I would be starting with an empty shell of a team and a few key consultants in place. This is where the chosen family learnings came into play. As I negotiated my final package, for the first time in my career, I did not focus on my salary, benefits, or bonus first. Instead, I asked for carte blanche empowerment and support in hiring my senior team and building the organization structure for success. I asked for salary, bonus, and title support for five senior vice presidents in various functions: franchise, creative, retail/e-commerce, global licensing, and international.

In the background, I was having lunches, dinners, and coffee dates with people in my life who I had worked with previously and one executive who was serving as a consultant at Fox. Due to the major consolidations going on in the media and entertainment sector, there was talent available who I needed to hold on to until I could do something official. I just kept meeting and chatting and texting and telling these people, who trusted me, to hold on and NOT take any other role without talking to me first. This included a now famous three-hour lunch and shopping spree in London when we were ceremoniously uninvited to meetings at Licensing Expo in fall 2018. After booking our trips last-minute to attend transition meetings to the new Dreamworks ownership, all our meetings were cancelled at the last minute when we landed. What else to do but retail therapy and long lunches and talk about the future?

Let me be clear, the only reason this worked is we were already a working and functional family-like unit. Trust, confidentiality, mutual respect all played in our favor. Five of us worked together at Disney, four of us at Dreamworks, and the other two were consultants whom I was asking to come back to a permanent role in corporate media and entertainment. I worked out my personal contract and the deal terms for the five senior leadership roles simultaneously. Fox HR was so supportive and remarkably nimble and flexible. I think my new bosses had something to do with that behind the scenes. My announcement appeared in the trade press the third week of January 2017. I announced the five senior vice presidents exactly one week later. The industry was on fire! It was so much fun to see and hear the reactions from our peers and competitors. It had never been done before and instantly changed the morale and culture of Fox Consumer Products.

We had so much work to do, but we were doing it as a team and a talented work family. We attacked our challenges and opportunities with vigor and focus. We worked so hard, but we always found time to laugh and celebrate small wins. Our past experiences and relationships allowed us to move with speed and efficiency. We talked in shorthand and quickly were ending each other's thoughts. Our eye contact communication was legendary.

I was living and leading the perfect example of chosen family. Tim, Kirk, Eva, Ann, Erin, and I were able to build a high-performance team and culture, and entered many new and innovative deals and partnerships.

Other than my Disney Store tenure, I was having the time of my life. I truly loved the first 12 months of that job. We had never strategized and merchandised teen and adult franchises before, but now did so for *The Simpsons, Bob's Burgers, American Horror Story,* and so many others. We got to stretch our creative wings and experiment with so many fun projects, including working on classics like *Home Alone, Die Hard, The Sandlot,* and *Buffy the Vampire Slayer.* In fact, one of my favorite stories about creative marketing and initiative has to do with our intern Spencer, and our PR/communications head Craig. They arranged to ship dirt from the original baseball diamond from *The Sandlot* to use as a "gift with purchase" promotion. One day, I walked past a conference room in our office, only to see Spencer in gloves and a mask, methodically filling small tins with dirt! We sold out of that dirt, and made a community of fans very happy. That was the energy and dedication we had in that early culture. I thought I was going to be there for years, and that I would groom my successor from direct reports. Little did I know how wrong those assumptions would prove to be.

Our chosen family relationship was the only thing that survived the next 16 months of that job.

Around Thanksgiving 2017, rumors started that Fox was for sale and Disney was acquiring certain assets it was allowed to based on antitrust considerations. I have learned in Hollywood that where there is smoke, there is fire, and I had to instantly dive into message management and team communication to keep the business in motion. Employees, retailers, licensees, and promotional partners were all abuzz with the rumor mill updating daily. I was managing phone calls, texts, and emails from around the world, with "no comment" and literally no knowledge.

"Business as usual" became code for "put on a poker face and keep smiling." Again, my work family unit kicked into high gear. We were in constant communication and contact. We compared rumors, searched for facts, actively managed the team, and waited for decisions that were out of our control. I admired my leadership's team ability to focus on the greater concern of the team, and not solely on their own futures. Finally, right before Christmas, Fox officially accepted Disney's offer and we were off to the races. The holiday breaks were somewhat crazy, and our team returned to the office in January 2018 with fear, anticipation, curiosity, and many questions. I think we had always viewed Fox as a buyer, not a seller, and we were still digesting the news and what the future may look like.

I had managed the Dreamworks acquisition by Comcast/NBC Universal previously, so I knew I had to put on my Big Boy leadership hat and work overtime on communication and active listening. My Mom had a favorite saying that would ring in my ears, "That is why they pay you the big bucks, honey." Very Midwestern work ethic—no whining, no crying, no complaining. Just put your head down and do the work. The "merger," which was actually an acquisition, took over 18 months. There were so many regulatory issues and hurdles, and the pieces of the company were separated into "Old Fox" and "New Fox." We were caught in the middle, but our function was considered Old Fox, so we knew we were being acquired and transferred to

Disney. It was a long and painful roller coaster ride of emotions, misinformation, rumor management, and angst. It was very difficult for a leader who prided himself on controlling the controllable and for getting teams to focus and perform. Every meeting literally had a Disney elephant in the room.

Almost instantly, I was transformed into a HR generalist and outplacement specialist. I felt, at times, like the Dutch boy with my finger holding back the water in the dyke. I also felt a little like Lucy in the psychiatrist booth from *Peanuts*, as my office was a revolving door of counseling and listening sessions. When you are part of the acquired company, you automatically assume the incumbents in key roles at the acquiring company will get the plum assignments, and you and your team will be left fighting for scraps. In my case, I was 1,000% sure that there would not be a role for me at Disney, so I was able to focus on my team and their needs.

For the next year and a half, I met regularly with large groups, small groups, and individuals to talk about their needs and desires. With over 80 employees, I developed an Excel spreadsheet on which I kept track of our conversations and their goals. For example, some people definitely wanted to transfer to Disney. Others absolutely did not want to transfer, for a variety of reasons. Some wanted severance and a return to school, or an opportunity to move to a new industry. Some immediately began a job search and resigned without waiting to learn their fate. Some were passive and wanted to trust the process. It was a fascinating sociological study at times. I worked very hard to make each person feel like they were in control of their future; I did not want anyone playing a victim. That is my personality and my leadership style. You have already learned about my control focus earlier in this book.

As the time dragged on, it became increasingly difficult to moti-
vate the staff and keep "business as usual." No company wants to
do a licensing deal with a company that will soon be controlled
by Disney, the largest licensor in the world. The industry correctly assumed Disney would change all deal terms, so they
stopped negotiating with us. Attendance became an issue. Attri-
tion became an issue. Focus became an issue. It was hard to discipline anyone, given the circumstances. My amazing assistants,
John P. and Dan "Dot," were rocks throughout and played a
pivotal role in keeping me connected to the scuttlebutt. Our
operations manager, Jared, who had worked with me since
Claire's days, did a wonderful job of keeping workflow "on task."
Jared is a treasured member of my chosen family. He is someone
I hired to be an EA for a CEO and has turned into one of the
most honest and authentic friends in my life. Talk about a truth
teller . . . he is an honest and unflinching brother and keeps me
sane and focused. At Dreamworks, he was dubbed "human
Xanax" for his ability to calm my nerves and my tendency to
overreact to certain situations.

My senior team kicked into high gear during this period as well.
We had no choice. The team was depending on us, and we had
to bifurcate our minds to focus on them, while simultaneously
considering our individual options post-merger. I simply cannot
imagine going through this event without their talent, expertise,
humor, and support. It supports my thesis that your chosen family is, at times, more important than your natural family. You are
able to keep your sanity and function at a higher level, if you
have the right unit in place. I wish I could fully paint the picture
of this period in words. I had never experienced anything like
that before, and I hope I never do again.

There is one amazing, illustrative, and embarrassing story I want to share with you. It is meant to show the support of the chosen family, but it means I have to expose a weakness and a mistake I made to illustrate the learning. Please enjoy my vulnerability and humanness! You can also enjoy a sneak peek into the realities of large corporate takeovers.

As part of the transaction and transition process, our leadership team had to travel to the Disney Consumer Products campus in Glendale, California, for communication, education, and project management meetings. There was a series of two- to three-hour meetings over a number of months. They were awkward, surreal, and somewhat demeaning. I returned to a building I had exited in 2012, visiting in conference rooms routinely used for strategic leadership meetings in my past. As I entered the building, I would run into people whom I knew and had worked for me a full six or seven years after my departure. Of course, it was great to see them, but it felt weird and uncomfortable, as I was there as an invited guest of an acquired business unit. I loved being warmly greeted, but it felt so awkward in front of the new Disney leadership team and our hosts.

The meeting dynamics were just strange. My direct report team on one side of the table with the Disney Consumer Products leadership team on the other side of the table and a variety of observers scattered around the periphery of the room. The respective legal heads were all present to keep us on task and in the lane of acceptable topics and conversation. After fractured and awkward introductions and greetings, we dove into the core of the meeting, which was supposed to be knowledge transfer and research. In reality, they were a slightly tortuous review of

every decision we had made in our time at Fox. Some of the
Disney people on the other side of the table had actually worked
with and for me at some point. I attempted to use our personal
connections to swing the meeting back to a more positive and
collegial knowledge transfer atmosphere to no avail. Our team
did our best to remain calm, collaborative, and positive in our
delivery. I truly was committed to a seamless knowledge transfer,
and I wanted as many people on our team to get Disney offers
as possible. I believed if these meetings were successful, that
would help more people on our team achieve their goals.

One meeting was particularly draining, and it was hard for me
not to feel attacked and demeaned. The lead Disney attendee
kept looking at his watch and phone, and told us we were wast-
ing his time without better numbers and data. To be clear, we
had been told by Fox legal that it was not appropriate to share
numbers, other than what were in the "clean data room," but
that did not seem to matter. There was an appalling lack of
respect for us and our work, and I felt embarrassed and protective of my team. The Disney team kept asking the same questions over and over, in slightly different formats and it was just
draining, and honestly, annoying. I was tired and weak, and in
my mind, I was saying "This is torture, I cannot f---ing take this
anymore." In reality, I slapped the conference table and said it
aloud. My team member Eva quietly leaned over to me and said
in a whisper, "You said that aloud." I was mortified. The air in
the room was still. I had never been in a meeting like this and I
had lost it publicly.

To my team members' credit, they stood up and asked for a
break and got me out of the room. I had hit my capacity for
handling the stress and the fake interactions. I went to the men's
room and splashed water on my face and looked at myself in the

mirror. I knew I had to go back in and apologize, which I did. It was so humbling, and I felt so immature and stupid. This was not the kind of leader I had become, but I slipped back into old insecurities and habits. Subconsciously, I was struggling with the fact that Disney did not "want" my participation and it dredged up so many bad memories from my exit in 2012. I entered the room and sincerely apologized. Then, we moved forward. The learning of this anecdote is that my chosen work family supported me unconditionally and got me out of a sticky situation. I am still grateful today and I apologized for putting them in that situation. We did have some good laughs over dirty martinis and sauvignon blanc at the bar after that meeting!

★ ★ ★

I was privileged throughout my career to have worked with some amazing executive assistants. I remember the first role where I had an EA assigned to me. It was in January 2001, when I arrived at Disney. At first, I was not sure what I was supposed to do with this kind of support. Of course, I knew scheduling and expense reports made sense. Initially, I had my personal calendar separated from my work calendar. Then, I met and worked with the wonderful Joanne M., who taught me so much and became like a sister to me . . . a true member of the chosen family. She immediately told me I had to trust her and let her into my personal life and plans, mainly to avoid scheduling conflicts. I quickly learned that this was wisest move in my life, and she became a rock for me. I never asked her to run personal errands, but she was amazing at anticipating my "hangry" moments and cutting them off before they happened. She helped me plan so many personal and professional events, and made me look so smart and proactive. In a company like Disney, she was a valuable asset who worked the assistant hotline to keep me abreast of important news and insights. I would not have made it almost 12 years at Disney without her talent and professionalism.

★ ★ ★

Another huge learning in my life has been the importance and presence of authentic male friendship. As I look at my chosen family, I am struck by the amazing men in my life, both straight and gay, who influence me so greatly and make me a better leader and friend. I have built my own "Band of Brothers" to not only enrich my personal life so greatly, but also to make me a better man overall, and thus, a better business executive. I think part of this desire for male bonding is because I never had a brother. I always wished I had an older brother as I felt I was supposed to be a middle child in the birth order. I would have benefitted greatly from the support and mentorship of an older sibling. There is nothing more important to me than time with my "boys." Gay, straight, and bisexual men who represent the spectrum of male sexual identity and experience. Jay, Gerardo, Michael, Carson, Brendon, Jared, Fabrice, Billy, Paul, Justin, and more keep me grounded and honest and allow me to just be me. That is a gift. Each of them teaches me something different and all of them make me laugh and relax. Nothing can replace that.

Many of my friends in my childhood and teen years were two or three years older than I was, and I was naturally drawn to a more mature friend base. These men of varied ages and backgrounds are truly brothers to me. I have officiated weddings, been a godfather, become a "guncle," and laughed and cried with them all. Their strengths and talents are awe inspiring. I also think this is why I joined a fraternity at Indiana University. I was a proud frater of Tau Kappa Epsilon and enjoyed the male camaraderie and community. I participated fully and have life-long friendships from my pledge class and with my Big Brother and his family. I was honored to be named TKE Alumnus of the Year in 2010 by the national fraternity and enjoyed working with the new members of our chapter when I could. Community, tribe, family, unity, unconditional. My favorite people in the world are my straight male friends who are comfortable enough in their own sexuality to love and embrace me fully. Each of them teaches me in his own unique way.

I recently heard the term *found family* and I love that descriptor for this discussion as well. It reflects again how blessed I am to have such an amazing chosen, found, or community family that I have built over the years. It also made me think how my chosen family has led me back to my natural family and created interesting ties on their own. My sister is great friends with many of my college friends and their extended families. My dear friend Anne Marie and her family are also close to my sister and Mom. I love spending time with my friends' parents, siblings, and children. All types of families go through ups and downs, but I recognize the value of the connective tissue even more now. Intersected stories, moments of truth, wisdom and guidance, truth telling all originate at this foundation.

Finally, I cannot fully address this learning of chosen family without talking about my partners with whom I have shared this journey. I have had four long-term relationships in my life. My first relationship lasted 14 years and ended amicably, but we parted because I put my career and my ambition in front of his needs and dreams. He was an amazing and gentle soul, but I sacrificed that situation to chase my career. It was not fair to him, and in the moment, I did not fully acknowledge what was occurring, but

I hurt him unnecessarily. My second relationship lasted seven years and was passionate, tumultuous, and exciting, and ultimately, unsustainable. He was an intelligent, handsome, and learned artist and designer, but he also had demons I could not overcome.

I was at the peak of my career as president of Disney Stores, when I met my third partner. He was a friend I had known for nine years before we ever went on a date, so when we actually acknowledged the spark, it was like a relationship on steroids. We were very much in love and fought very hard for the national right to marry. When the Supreme Court decision came down, we immediately planned our wedding for April 2015. I never expected to be legally married in my lifetime. That weekend is one of the fondest memories of my life, as our worlds and families came together for a magical three-day event in Palm Springs. Sadly, that marriage ended in a 2019 separation and divorce in 2020, during the height of the Covid-19 pandemic. That unexpected and difficult period has completely changed me as a person, and in hindsight, made me a better and more empathetic leader. I am grateful we have remained friends and genuinely care about each other, but learned we could not be a healthy and mutually supportive partnership.

Leaving the marriage and changing everything, especially during the lockdown and isolation, was the hardest thing I have ever done in my life. I have never been so low, depressed, and alone. To be clear, I did not have a choice. I would have stayed married for the rest of my life, but my husband asked me for a divorce and admitted that he needed to move on in his life without me. I was devastated and tried to change his mind, but then my self-care needs kicked in and we negotiated a settlement. There is nothing that can prepare you for the end of a marriage or relationship. You lose friends, you lose your partner's family, you lose self-esteem, and you lose belief. It was really hard on my family as they had grown very close to my husband. My Mom could not process it all. I argued with my Mom because I felt like she wasn't taking care of me. I called her a narcissist because she seemed incapable of understanding what I was going through and how I felt. She actually told me I would be fine because I was so strong and I always bounced back. I screamed at her . . . I told her I was not fine. I told her I was devastated and cracked and felt like I was going crazy . . . even that did not wake her up. My sister played peacemaker, and we are fine today, but the wound is present today and seems to be permanent. I also recognized the pattern of addiction that I had been dealing with my entire life repeating itself in this situation. The caretaker in me had run out of capacity.

In hindsight, it is amazing how fast your world changes when your husband tells you he wants to separate and eventually divorce. When we fought so hard for marriage equality, I never stopped to consider that we were also fighting for divorce equality. I never imagined the end of that relationship. When we walked down that aisle, I thought it was forever. When it abruptly ended, I had no choice but to grieve, cry, scream, blame, and slowly heal. It is not that our marriage was perfect, and I cannot say it was totally surprising when he told me, but it still hurt like hell and was scary. I was 55, transitioning out of a powerful corporate role, and had to find new housing as part of the divorce settlement. I could not believe my marriage and my corporate Big Media career were ending simultaneously. Mental health professionals always talk about the major stressors in life: relationship change, career change, moving homes, and death. I was living through them all, and then add in Covid isolation. It is a wonder I did not crack or just give up. I was angry, confused, hurt, and broken. I had failed in so many ways. Failure and feeling out of control are not emotions or realities I would like to experience again, but it is real.

What I learned about myself in this tumultuous period is I have a strong ability to "compartmentalize." Somehow, I was able to complete my work at Fox, transition the business to Disney, sell real estate, plan my next chapter, and process the divorce. I am not honestly 100% sure why or if this is learned behavior? Maybe it was compartmentalizing my life early in my career and my coming out process. I think I had always learned to divide my brain space into little boxes on a shelf, and to only open the relevant ones when necessary. I know that sounds odd. I wish I could train people or explain to people how I did it, but I always felt like I did not have a choice. I was going to move and push forward. I was going to grow, but I knew I needed to heal first.

Thanks to my family and friends, I was able to escape to Northern Michigan to rest and recuperate and lick my wounds. In fact, I was blessed to share the cross-country drive from California to Michigan with Taj, the son of Linda and Lee. Taj shared the driving with me, took care of the dogs, and listened to my stories without judgment or visible signs of boredom! I also listened to him and his plans for his future and it made me feel optimistic again! Driving cross country during a pandemic lockdown could be a whole separate chapter, but suffice to say it was an adventure. I spent the summer of 2020 alone in Michigan with my books, my dogs, my journal, and Lake Michigan. At one point, I looked in the mirror of my bathroom and had a Brene Brown and Oprah Winfrey moment. I literally looked at myself and said, "You are OK. In fact, you are perfect. God has a plan and you are exactly where you are supposed to be right now. You may not understand it, you may not like it, but you need to trust the Higher Power. If you spend the rest of your life alone, you are fine. You are surrounded by loving family and friends and that will sustain you. You do not need a partner to complete you. You are a fully formed human being and you need to accept your situation with grace and gratitude." I prayed, I meditated, and I journaled daily, as I learned to accept my new reality and my life situation. I could have never planned for or anticipated what was going on in my life at that time, but I had no choice, except to adapt and stay open to what was coming.

Which brings me to my present-day chapter. After learning to love and appreciate myself during the solitude of pandemic separations, I met my current partner on an online dating service, and we are now building our lives together. So, yes, I did go to the apps during the pandemic! I was only on a particular service because two of my straight male friends told me about their own success in finding a life partner. I was very skeptical, but I did end up enjoying the process. Fate also intervened, as I mistakenly selected 500 miles in my search parameter on the app, rather than 50, which is how I was served up my Atlanta connection and gift of the unique and soulful man I found. Technology and doing the app without my reading glasses resulted in a joy- and laughter-filled relationship. He is intelligent, handsome, passionate, funny, charming, and has a fun-filled and gratitude-focused approach to life. He is educated and talented, and has the type of job that makes a real difference in the world. He is a pediatric emergency room doctor, and watching him work, especially during the pandemic, is a tremendous source of inspiration for me. He is an optimist and ambitious and so good at this job, I could not be more proud of him and the impact he makes on families and the community.

I know that I just disclosed a bunch of personal information, but I felt it was important to share this personal narrative. It is my authentic story and everyone needs to understand that we all have our wins and losses. What I want you to learn and understand is simply this: NEVER sacrifice your personal happiness and relationships for career growth. Learn early to prioritize your partnership, marriage, boyfriend, girlfriend, and other friendships and NEVER take them for granted. Wake up every day and say a prayer of gratitude for these people. Make authentic connections with people you love, trust, and respect. And make sure they make you smile and laugh and relax!

To that point, it feels only right to thank my parents publicly and to also forgive them. I now understand how much they loved me and how they did the best they truly could with the information and resources available to them. I was not an easy child to raise and I am sure I overwhelmed them often! As I said earlier, I was a unicorn in a land full of donkeys, and I know I challenged them constantly. Today, I can say with immense gratitude that they did grow, change, and come to understand me and my needs and my life. Still, like other episodes and people in my life, I needed to go through a formal "letting go" process and forgiveness ritual. This process took coaching and I worked with an incredible man who had me write a long letter to my Mom and Dad . . . forced me to get it all down on paper and never give it to them. Instead, we burned that paper in an amazing, spiritual, and healing ceremony.

Forgiveness heals. Families, regardless of how they occur, make you better. They love you unconditionally. They celebrate your growth and successes. They will tell your truth and call you on your BS, always keeping you real and humble. You will be a better leader because of them. Define FAMILY however it works for you, but do not ever feel like you are alone in the world.

5 | How to Define *Enough?*

I spent most of my life chasing something elusive and unique. I wanted to be "successful." I honestly am not ever sure what it is, but with hindsight, I think I started this quest at a very early age. Remember, I was raised in a blue-collar, middle-class, Midwestern family. We were taught very early about the value of money and how to save and be frugal. I seem to have been born with a certain taste and aesthetic that always had me searching for "more." I also am certain I was trying to fill some void in myself and was trying to wrap myself in the comforts of newness and materialism. I sought happiness and validation through acquisitions and external stimuli, which is actually a very hollow and temporary fix.

My parents, especially my father, taught us a very early life lesson about the difference between what you want and what you need. He drilled that into us on many occasions. For me, it usually surfaced around back-to-school shopping time. In those days, the ritual of back-to-school shopping began about four weeks before the start of the school year, which was always the Tuesday after Labor Day in Ohio. Our family practice began with a review of what still fit or was good enough from last year. My personal process began with a review of teen magazines and catalogs. My parents would discuss and set a budget, and that money had to cover everything . . . shoes, backpacks, clothes, underwear, socks . . . everything! Even at a young age, like nine, I would try to argue for a bigger budget! My Dad started to educate me fully on this topic as I was entering 4th grade. I was becoming conscious of what was "cool," and my shopping list looked different that year. I had saved my allowance for the shopping outings, but it was obvious to my parents that I was short of the funds necessary for my expectations. Dad took this opportunity to say, "You have champagne tastes on a beer budget," and to introduce the Fielding family ledger concept.

The family ledger was an old-fashioned accounting book he kept in his desk drawer. He started a page labeled "Jimmy." It was a physical record of the difference between what you "want" and what you "need." For example, that year I wanted Calvin Klein or Jordache jeans, but the budget allowed for Sears Tuffskins. There was about a $30 differential between the options. My Dad would loan me the difference and note that transaction in the ledger. Entries would include the date of purchase, the item description, and the delta between the cost of my choice versus the "approved" option. If I received extra allowance or birthday money, I could pay down on the account and that would all be recorded. So began a lifelong recordkeeping that continued (without interest!) until I was in my late 20s. Thank goodness it was not an interest-bearing account.

I realize now that he was educating us in a very tangible way about the value of money and hard work. In fact, I paid off my Dad's ledger right before my 30th birthday, as I was preparing to buy my first house. It was a debt that needed to be cleared for our relationship health and my psyche. I still hear his voice in every major purchase I make to this day: "Jimmy, do you really need a Rolex . . . I have been wearing my Timex for 30 years," or "The Range Rover is nice, but there are much more value-oriented SUVs on the market and maybe you should buy American-made." I appreciate his guidance and wisdom, even from the great hereafter, and it does make me think and has taught me a lot about myself and how I navigate in this world. Dad's voice is in my ear with every major purchase.

I have an interesting side story about the family ledger and my sister. Two weeks before she was getting married in our hometown of Toledo, Ohio, I called to check in and gently remind her about paying off her ledger before the wedding so she would begin her married life with a clean slate. Of course, she asked, "Do you really think Dad remembers?" I laughed and said I bet he could recite the current running total at a moment's notice! I even offered to loan her the money to get it off of Dad's book. Needless to say, she walked down the aisle Dad's-ledger-book debt-free.

To this day, it sometimes feels like my sister and I, who are so close and similar in many ways, are from different families when it comes to "stuff" and what motivates our purchase behavior. I am champagne; she is wine coolers. I am Ritz-Carlton; she is Hampton Inn. She, of course, loves the finer things in life, but she never needed them the way that I did and still seem to need to this day. At times, I was jealous of her. She was so appreciative of the simple joys of life, while I was on a constant hunt for the next new or big thing.

Restaurants and food are a great example of our relationship. When we were young, every Saturday was Grandpa and Nana Farrell's lunch adventure day. Every other week, I got to choose where we went, alternating selections with Jill. This began when we were really young, maybe three and six years old. Our grandfather always appreciated the finer things in life. He was always dressed up in a sport coat and tie, and we always were in our finest for these outings. On my weeks, I routinely chose a fancy restaurant with finely dressed wait staff, Shirley Temple cocktails, appetizers, and after-dinner dessert and drinks. My sister always chose McDonald's because she was obsessed with their filet of fish sandwiches. . . . I think you can spot the difference here. It got to the point where I was bargaining with her, almost begging her, to choose anything but fast food. I bribed her with candy, little toys, and doing her chores. I considered it a small victory if she actually chose Red Lobster or Olive Garden for her week, but that was still well below my lofty standards, even as an eight-year-old.

Subconsciously, I understood that her approach was acceptable; it was just not "enough" for me. I was Rolex; she was Timex. Same parents, same house, same morals and ethics and education . . . completely different aesthetic, tastes, wants, and needs. I had some kind of void that I was attempting to fill that she did not seem to have. Looking back, I realize how much my grandfather's tastes and styles influenced me. My Dad never really liked or respected him and referred to him as a show-off or snob. My Dad always pointed out that he did not own anything . . . that he and Nana spent all their money on stuff trying to impress other people and live above their station in life. My Dad thought he was a fake. I resolved that I could do both, however: be stable and save and plan for the future AND indulge in the luxuries of life.

I think the queer community is really hard and overly focused on the most superficial aspects of life. Sadly, our community can be our own most severe judges and harshest critics. I swear that the term FOMO (fear of missing out) started in our community. Especially in LA/West Hollywood, we have taken "keeping up with the Joneses" to extremes. Your body, your car, your house, your clothes, your friends . . . sadly, we judge and make assumptions on how you present consistently. I have seen it cause crippling anxiety and have felt it myself. Even though I lived and worked successfully in Los Angeles for over 20 years, I always felt the pressure. I constantly compared myself to some invisible standard that I instinctively understood but could not fully identify, but you knew and felt its presence.

As a visible queer executive, I was overly conscious of my house, my car, my clothes, and where I vacationed. It was the ultimate status symbol, especially in the queer community, to have a second home in Palm Springs. I loved the community there, but, again, felt the struggle to fit in properly. There was that underlying "less than" insecurity that blossomed in childhood, gnawing away at me. It always felt like I was running to just keep up, and I would achieve something and then ask myself, "What next?" Was I ever done? Could I simply enjoy everything I had and stop there? I thought I just had great drive and ambition, but I think I was filling a gaping void inside and trying to fit in and receive external validation. I am not blaming my community or finger pointing. I am just simply saying I wish I had this knowledge and insights when I was younger, as it would have saved me a lot of internal grief and doubt. I always felt like I was on the outside looking in . . . having to work twice as hard to prove I was supposed to be part of the group.

Do not even get me started on the body image and standards of beauty and fitness in our community. It can really be devastating and harmful to your self-esteem. I wish we could elevate and celebrate the diversity within our community more easily and more often. I know I sound judgmental and overly harsh, just please know I am judging myself the most of all. I want to help our community be more accepting and more diverse and more aware of this ridiculous pressure. As a community, we have dealt with judgment and harassment and being made to feel different and unworthy of love our entire lives. We should not be creating divisions or cliques within our own community. We should always be coming together for the greater common cause.

★ ★ ★

It got to a stage where this constant striving for something new or better was just my normal mode of operation. I began to think it was just the way I was wired, and it had made me successful, at least in the eyes of our community. Inside, though, it often felt incomplete. and empty. With the help of my executive coach and therapist, I started to peel back the layers of my personality and identified that I had severe ethical and moral conflicts with my situation in corporate America. I was chasing the bigger job and the bigger payday at the expense of my own happiness. I was fundamentally selling pieces of my soul to keep up the facade of success and it was eating away at me.

I knew I was very good at my jobs, and I deserved to be rewarded, but some of the roles I took and the people I had to work with made me sacrifice my core values and beliefs. When I am passionate and focused about a role, there is no stopping me. If I feel like I am just 'punching a clock," it is really challenging. It is a little bit like "dimming my light," which I wrote about earlier, but there is a difference. This life lesson is about spending time with yourself, listening to yourself, learning about yourself, and loving yourself properly in order to define your goals and success. Do not let society or someone else define your happiness or definition of success.

Please hear me. I love my experiences and travels around the world. I love eating in all kinds of special restaurants globally. I love five-star experiences and hotels. I will pay big money for the best seats at the theater. I treasure my art collection and can tell you the story of each piece and how it came into my life. I appreciate exquisitely tailored clothing, accessories, and shoes. I love innovative and high-quality, classic and modern home decor and architecture. I am grateful for all the places, stuff, and people I have been exposed to in my life.

I want you to understand, however, this very important learning. This is a piece of wisdom 57-year-old Jim would love to share with 24-year-old Jim. Do these things, buy these things, travel around the world because you WANT to, not because you NEED to or you think it makes your life more interesting to others. Make yourself an interesting life and find joy and satisfaction in small pleasures. Please understand, young Jim, the critical difference in this advice. You cannot fill voids, insecurities, and gaps in your happiness with stuff. It is a temporary fix and becomes an almost uncontrollable addiction of sorts. External validation and social media likes are temporary and fleeting.

You must address your core happiness and desires first and learn how to practice gratitude and appreciation for what you have. Stay humble, remember and honor your roots, and you can always strive for new and exciting adventures, but keep it all in perspective please. You are enough. You are worthy. You are amazing. You bring joy to many people in your life. Take. A. Breath. Stop and smell the roses. Life is too damn short to be constantly searching for your next hit of external validation. Get off that treadmill. And keep smiling!

6

May We Leave Our Corner of the World a Better Place than We Found It

I was raised in a family of philanthropists, volunteers, political activists, and people who wanted to make a difference. I really did not realize that until I was in my 40s and was starting to give back my personal time, talent, treasure, and testimony to foundations and causes that brought out my passion. My grandfather, father, and uncles were all Shriners, proud members of the Zenobia Shrine in Toledo, Ohio. They all participated in a variety of subgroups within that organization; I always saw the social aspect of the membership, but I underestimated the amount of money they raised for children's hospitals. My mother was the consummate involved school parent, volunteering for everything she could, and serving as an officer in the Mother's Club. Both of my parents were involved in leadership roles in our boat club, our neighborhood association, and various Toledo-based fundraising initiatives.

From an early age, we had the "clean out the toy closet" ritual in preparation for every Christmas and Santa's arrival. My sister and I were taught to appreciate what we had, and to always realize there were other people less fortunate than we were. That moral lesson ran deep in my family on both sides. My favorite aunt and godmother, Aunt Pat, and her family were the wealthy relatives in our family. I remember going to their beautiful house for the key holidays, and even there, we would collect food for shelters and gifts for charity. There was not a specific education on what philanthropy was, but we understood early on we had a responsibility to help others and to not act in a selfish manner. It was just part of my upbringing. I thought everyone did this; we did not openly talk about the fact we did these things, we just did them.

I was born an old soul. For the first three months of my life, I actually looked like a little old man. My Dad nicknamed me

"Mr. Magoo" because I looked like the old man cartoon character. It was a family story that my Dad looked at me in the hospital nursery and told them to "put me back in" to finish baking as I looked so old and wrinkly! At three months, my incessant eating kicked in and I filled out nicely. My psyche, however, was and is still that of a wizened older man. I believe in reincarnation and definitely feel like I have lived a few lives before this one.

There was a movie that starred Jodie Foster called *Little Man Tate*. Her son in that movie has an inordinate amount of intelligence and empathy for world affairs and it overwhelms him daily. He is a sad and serious soul in the movie who tries to fix things he has zero control or influence to accomplish. At times, I exhibited those behaviors. My parents constantly tried to teach me the difference between knowledge, caring, and worrying, but it was in vain. I do not remember ever really playing without fear, abandon, or awareness of the situation I was in at that time. I wish I could have been more innocent and carefree, but I was always aware of the repercussion and consequences of my actions and decisions. No one would ever have called me a risk taker or a carefree kid.

I always have felt, and will continue to feel, that I have a burden and expectation to make things better in my world, family, and community. It is not a sense of arrogance or entitlement or confidence that I have all the answers. It is, in fact, quite the opposite. I am horribly insecure at times and worry more often than I should about the state of the world and our communities. I just have this innate sense I am supposed to help in any way I can. As I said earlier, the theme of my National Honor Society graduation speech was "May we leave our corner of the world a little better than we found it." I delivered that at 18 years old. Now,

40+ years later, I am still following that mantra. I just wish I learned how to relax and enjoy the journey more as a younger man.

I began my adult journey of giving back in my early 30s when I arrived in San Francisco. Gap Inc. was a very generous corporate citizen in the city and Bay Area, and I could see the company impact in many different ways. I also admired how the Fisher Family Foundation, the founding Gap family, used its resources to create change in the community. Working at Gap HQ in Embarcadero was like visiting a modern art museum every day. Amazing art and sculpture installations throughout the offices was something I had never experienced before. It really stoked my imagination and passion for art and living with art in my home.

I arrived in San Francisco and the AIDS crisis was over 10 years old and still ravaging our community. We got our first rental in the Castro district, so it was a natural for me to start volunteering there. I delivered meals for Project Angel Food and worked to raise money for the Aids Quilt tour. I also started to support community theater in small ways. There was never a conscious moment where I said, "It is time to volunteer." Again, I had a family history of volunteering and participating in our community, but we never called it anything except giving back. It was expected of us. The AIDS crisis was devastating. Living in San Francisco meant I saw the impacts daily and I attended way too many funerals and memorial services.

Through my volunteer work for the cause, I met many of the first true "allies" I had ever seen. I came to marvel at the support of the straight extended family that leapt to the needs of our community. Many of them came because they were impacted by the disease in their work or family, but many came because they were caring and compassionate people. AIDS was not and is not a gay disease, but in the 1980s and 1990s, it certainly felt that way. I got to meet Dr. Anthony Fauci and Dr. Mathilde Krim in this period through my work and small donations. It was fascinating to watch Dr. Fauci navigate the Covid-19 crisis all of these years later, but I had witnessed his intelligence, strength, and compassion firsthand in San Francisco. I learned that every small donation and gesture made a difference, and I carried that with me into all of my charitable work. Again, it was part of our family history and heritage.

I have to share a pride-filled story about my Dad, James F. Fielding. He retired from the Toledo, Ohio, fire department in 1990 at the age of 50 with 27 years of service and a nice pension. My sister graduated from college, and four weeks later, my parents settled in a nice newly built home in Port St. Lucie, Florida, on the east coast. At first, my Dad was retired, almost comatose. He did not play golf, or fish, or play cards. He basically read voraciously, listened to Rush Limbaugh on the radio, and played with his dog. Honestly, we were worried about him, and he was driving my Mom crazy as he was constantly underfoot and "around." They were not used to being together that much, so she encouraged him to find ways to get out of the house. He found his calling by attending their neighborhood association meetings and getting involved in local issues and politics. He had always been very politically aware and astute but could not really participate due to his civil service role. He rose to be president of his neighborhood association and regularly attended city council meetings in that role. He always did his research and was prepared and vocal.

Suddenly, he was running for mayor of a 90,000-person city! He won and began his term full of vim and vigor and vision to address the issues of their quickly growing city. He was committed to building more schools and services, but was very conscious of controlling costs and taxes, as so many residents were on a fixed income. He dealt with wildfires, garbage issues, and alligator attacks. It was a very time-consuming and all-encompassing role. When he ran for reelection, his campaign materials mentioned his family, and I was very worried about my impact as a "single" man who was living out and about. He never hesitated including me in any materials or interviews and that made me realize how far we had come as a family.

During his reelection campaign, he also worked very hard on the reelection of Mark Foley to the U.S. House of Representatives. Dad was essentially his campaign lead in Port St. Lucie County and aligned with Foley's Republican agenda and experience. Mark Foley was thrust into national headlines due to an inappropriate intern relationship and eventually the disclosure of his homosexuality. I was shocked and very worried for my Dad but proud at the same time. My Dad defended him initially, not for the inappropriate behavior, but for his right to privacy about his sexuality. I could not believe he was willing to go on the record with his support. He kept encouraging the critics to focus on Mr. Foley's record, rather than his personal life. Ultimately, I think that this support cost my Dad votes, and he lost his reelection for mayor. After the results, more bad news came out about the inappropriate behavior and its impact on the victims, and I watched my Dad struggle with the information. He could not reconcile the man he knew, respected, and supported with the horrible actions that had been disclosed.

My Dad finished his term and returned to life as a private citizen after successfully transitioning the office to his successor. If you visit Port St. Lucie, you will see my Dad's name on the placard in City Hall, which was built and opened during his term. I could not have been more proud of him and his service. I was blown away by his personal growth and his willingness to take unpopular stands and support people he believed could make a difference in his community. I have so much respect now for mayors and city councils around the country and understand how important they are to people's lives and well-being. My Dad always taught me that "all politics are local" and that it was more important who our mayor, representative, and governor were than the president at times. He is and was a role model for me. Hard to believe how far we have come. I talk to my Dad all of the time and hear his voice in my head often. I miss him every day and wish we had him for a longer time on this earth. He was so smart, so wise, truly kind, and ultimately, passed away with grace and dignity. I hope he is proud of me every day.

★ ★ ★

My personal journey and charitable vision is based on my family's involvement and legacy and finding causes and organizations that I am passionate about. I am very proud to have served on the national and international boards for the Make-A-Wish Foundation, including a term as board chair. My father passed away while I was chair, and I was overwhelmed by the outpouring of support from the foundation. I also served on the national board for GLSEN (Gay, Lesbian, Straight Education Network), a group that forms and supports gay/straight alliances in middle and high schools. In addition, I have served on various local boards in my communities, like Kidspace Children's Museum and the American Red Cross. Serving on nonprofit boards is an excellent education for everyone, and a great way to build executive and leadership skills.

I think leaders should donate their time and talent and encourage and enable their teams to do the same. First, these groups do excellent and often underappreciated work. By using your skills and position in the community, you elevate their needs and stories. Second, nonprofits need to be constantly fundraising in new and innovative ways to fulfill their missions and the needs of the communities they serve. Third, you meet talented and committed executives from a wide variety of industries and build a network in your community. Finally, you see and feel the tangible impact of your efforts. I cried at every GLSEN and Make-A-Wish board meeting when we had the privilege to meet students from one of our programs or a Wish Kid and family. Borrowing from Truvy in *Steel Magnolias* "Laughter through tears is my favorite emotion" and working on charitable causes brought that to me tenfold.

I have devoted most of my time, talent, treasure, and testimony to my alma mater, Indiana University. I am engaged in many different groups on the Bloomington and Indianapolis campuses, and I am constantly stimulated by the interaction with the academic environment. Time with students and professors supports my quest for lifelong learning and gives me faith in our future with these young, brilliant minds at work in the world. I am especially proud of my work on the formation of the Queer Philanthropy Circle in 2019, a first of its kind affinity giving circle built by and for the queer community and its allies in our IU community. We have raised and granted over $750,000 in three short years, and I am confident our impact will be felt for years.

I also serve on the Foundation Board, the Black Philanthropy Circle, and the Women's Philanthropic Leadership Circle. It has been very educational to participate in these giving circles and to serve as a leader and a follower on a variety of committees. I love being an observer and analyzing the various approaches to meeting management, fundraising, and team structure. I realized that my queer leadership style is very much a blend of traditional male and female attributes, although I hesitate to use gender labels. In the Women's Philanthropic Leadership Circle, I am one of three men in a group of 50. I love the strong and passionate women I work with in this group. They have taught me about the importance of the Ts: Time, Talent, Treasure, Testimony, Trust, and Transparency.

I also have learned about the role of being an activist donor and advocate. Using my resources to support important causes brings me great joy. My filter on where to focus my energy is always a combination of knowing where I can add value with participation and where I am engaged and learning. A recent example is my financial and time donation to the LGBTQ+ Cultural Center on the Bloomington campus. I am passionately committed to the success of this center and completely understand the importance of a safe space on campus for our community. I wish I had the ability to access a place like this when I was on campus and struggling with my identity and mental health challenges.

I am also proud of the scholarship endowments we have created for the university. One was formed in honor of my Dad and enables students to study overseas in a country of their choosing as part of their education. The other scholarship fund enables overseas work internships.

All of this activity is not about personal recognition or honors. This is really about my desire to give back, reduce student debt, and enhance the educational journey of extraordinary students. When I get the opportunity to meet any of the scholarship recipients, I always get emotional and leave with optimism and hope for the future. I, myself, was a scholarship recipient, so it is really a full circle moment for me to fund these programs. I worked every year of college to help defray costs, but that meant I sacrificed some activities, so I enjoy removing barriers for current students. My work with the university overall is very fulfilling and supports my lifelong learning ambitions.

I also want to share my point of view on the incredible growth of corporate support for diversity programs and commitment to giving back in their communities. I applaud these efforts and find myself looking to work with companies that are authentically committed to giving back and using their position for positive change. I especially admire companies and corporate leaders who are unafraid to support difficult or controversial causes in the face of protests, shareholder revolts, and negative press.

The growth of Conscious Capitalism and consumers using their purchasing power to support or boycott certain companies has been surprising to me. The increase of Black History Month and Pride Month programs and products has also been an unexpected phenomenon. I am fully supportive of the awareness support and the visible efforts to play an ally role, for both their customers and their teams. I am cautious, though, to evaluate for what I call Rainbow Washing or DEI Slapping. I stay focused and research all of these programs to ensure year-round support, not just during the celebration months. Again, I am grateful and fully supportive, and at times shocked at the scope and number of programs. I just want to hold these companies accountable to their support for 365 days a year, and remind all of us why this product is even necessary. Visual representation and support is amazing . . . I just want to make sure it is authentic support, and not just a revenue opportunity. It is a fine line, but it is necessary to fully evaluate these initiatives to determine their ultimate impact on our community.

As a queer man and executive, I spent most of 2022 considering a very important type of giving back to our community. I talked to anyone in my circle who was willing to engage on this topic, and I read and researched anything relevant. I am addressing two types of giving back and activism: political donations and choosing where to live and pay my tax dollars. It is somewhat fascinating to me that I have been thinking about these topics so much in 2022, especially as a former political science major. First, I have always been a political donor. Even early in my career, I would send $5 or $10 a month to the Democratic Central Committee.

I was raised in a very Republican household and family by people who were committed to core Republican values of small government, strong military, the right to own a gun, and reducing national debt. As a voting and donating adult, I have primarily voted Democratic or Independent, based mostly on social issues. In reality, I am an Independent, a true centrist. I sometimes long for a legitimate third-party option, as I am socially progressive, yet fiscally conservative. Unfortunately, the polarization of American politics and the strengths of the Far Left and the Far Right make it difficult to navigate in this space. There does not seem to be a legitimate centrist path in politics today. I donate and support mainly Democratic candidates, as my commitment to social issues usually drives my vote decision making. I only support candidates who are Pro Choice, Pro Human Rights, Pro LGBTQ+ rights, and Pro Social Safety Net. I also am drawn to support nontraditional candidates, especially from historically underrepresented and marginalized communities.

While I agree with my father's mantra that all politics are local, I do choose to support national candidates and candidates for national office who can tip the balance of power in the Senate or the House of Representatives. I have been very cognizant of the federal judiciary appointments and the Supreme Court composition. I am also conscious of climate change, the national debt, and the stability of Social Security and Medicare. With all those considerations, it can be overwhelming and daunting, but it is part of my DNA to participate in the democratic process.

Since the 2016 election, I have spent long periods in an agitated and depressive state. Many times, I operated in a state of perpetual disbelief, but the realities of the Trump era are undeniable. I despair over the separation in our country, and the ongoing election denials and anger. Like many of you, I was in shock at the Capitol riots and the chaos of the transition to the Biden administration. For an involved control the controllable proponent, it can be debilitating. I have considered withdrawing into my bubble and cutting back on participation, but my moves to Indiana and then Georgia do not allow me to become passive. Living in California for almost 25 years makes you soft I have realized. You take so much for granted. You can insulate yourself in an echo chamber of like-minded individuals and close yourself off from the realities of national politics. A move back to the Midwest or the South does not really allow you to bubble yourself. So I find myself politically active and donating at a new rate, and trying to use my support and influence for positive change . . . trying to make the world a better place for our future. You have to participate when you live in a democracy. The closeness and surprising results of the November 2022 midterms showed that every vote matters.

In the last few months of 2022, I began discussing with my gay friends, especially gay couples, the topic of "where to live." Many of our friends are blessed to have economic security and choice, and for the first time in our lives, we are talking about where we want our state income and property taxes to be spent and used. When I was growing up, my parents chose where to live based on the quality of the public school system and proximity to work. They never considered moving as a political statement or to be in a community that felt safe and supportive. Now, anytime we meet up with our friends, the topic of potential moves is on the menu. We even have friends who are moving out of the country to find safety, security, and establish residency.

It saddens me to admit that while Atlanta is a liberal and progressive community, the state of Georgia is actually inhospitable, racist, and homophobic. I have to use my heightened awareness radar when I travel outside of the Atlanta metro area to ensure my safety. I am big, gay, and in an interracial relationship in the South, and that requires diligence. More importantly, do we want to live in a state that does not support a woman's right to choose or basic human rights and protections? Life is short and precious, and if I have a choice of where and how to live, should I choose to stay and fight? It makes me hesitate to invest in the community fully. It makes me second guess investment decisions in rental real estate and vacation home locations. I realize that these are "white man problems," but it is rooted in my commitment to community and my socialistic leanings.

I realize I have a choice. I am grateful I worked hard and was rewarded by having economic freedom through mobility. I worry, however, about the vast majority of people, especially queer and BIPOC people, who do not have choice or economic freedom. I feel for the young people in Texas, Indiana, and Oklahoma, for example. The entire queer community and our allies cannot only live in California, Oregon, Washington, New York, New Jersey, and DC. We cannot be forced into a segregated society again. There are so many forces separating us, but I am committed to fight for unifying ideas and positions. I will admit, though, it is very tiring and draining. It makes me sad and mad to even be thinking about this in 2022, but it is real. I listen, read, learn, and talk to anyone I can. I will continue the fight. I cannot stop my lifelong commitment to positive change now.

As I wrote this, I watched the results of the November 2022 midterm elections roll in and I was pleasantly surprised and cautiously optimistic about some of the results. Election deniers and MAGA Republicans lost most of their races. Women and young people came out and used their voices and votes with focused power. Of course, I live in Georgia now and we had a run-off for Senate, so we headed to the polls again in December to support democracy, women's rights, LGBTQ+ rights, and simple civility in politics. I want to acknowledge and thank the Democratic caucus in the House of Representatives for showing us how to lead with dignity and grace. Nancy Pelosi honored a commitment she made in 2018 to step aside four years later for a new generation of leadership. After the horrible attack on her husband, I am sure it cemented her decision. With one visionary decision, she and two other 80-year-olds who have served with wisdom and dedication stepped aside for new voices and insights. I hope other leaders in both parties watch and learn. Democracy is alive, but our work is never done. Democracy is a privilege, not a right.

In one of my current consulting roles, I work with a group of Ukrainians on an animated children's television show. Some of them are still living in Kyiv and deal with the daily bombings and challenging infrastructure as a result of Russia's war on their country and culture. Some have temporarily relocated to Spain, Poland, and Germany. We have regular video calls with them, when the power and technology allow. I am always struck by how positive and strong they are in the face of danger and uncertainty. They smile; they laugh; they share their stories, and I am blown away by their commitment to democracy and freedom for their country and community. I would love to capture their energy in a bottle and take it to all U.S. high schools civics or government 101 classes.

Learning #6 began in my family traditions and continues to evolve as I age and mature. One caring and compassionate voice can make a difference. Support democracy and VOTE and use your power wisely.

There are stories every day and everywhere of inspirational people making efforts to impact their communities in a positive way. The size of the effort does not matter; ripples in the water have ways of multiplying. Watch the young people in your life, as I see incredible sparks of innovation and commitment in their words and deeds.

We have much to learn and admire from the world around us. Just commit to leaving your piece of it better than you found it.

7 | Trust Your Jiminy Cricket . . . Learn to Listen to and Love Yourself

On the first day of cast member orientation at The Walt Disney Company, you are asked to share the story of your favorite Disney character. At Disney, all employees are referred to as "cast members," regardless of where you work, as everyone is part of the story and magic creation. This character is then included on your Disney name badge and follows you throughout your career. It is an excellent and innovative way to connect new hires to the culture and heritage of the company, to create easy initial conversations with fellow cast members, and to learn something about a person's personality. It is storytelling at its finest! As an executive at Disney, I was legendary for my ability to remember people's names and favorite characters. I mostly remembered their stories and that would help me recall their names. To be honest, I also had good eyesight and could spot the information on their badge as they were walking toward me! It became a kind of game with cast members at Disney Stores globally. Some of them would ask for multiple name badges with different favorite character options, depending on their mood. Some wanted a favorite villain and a favorite hero, again showcasing their mood that day, for example, Cruella De Vil and Blue Fairy. Some people wanted to have a "classic" and a "modern," for example, Cinderella and Eve from *Wall-E*. For me, this was a very easy choice and I had stuck with this answer since my childhood. My favorite Disney character is Jiminy Cricket.

Pinocchio is one of the first Disney movies I remember seeing in a theater with my mother. I vividly remember being simultaneously excited and scared. I realize now that the themes and the suspense in that movie are very mature and sophisticated, but I loved it anyway. Jiminy Cricket is Pinocchio's best friend and conscience. He serves as a centering influence and has a very strong moral fiber. I recognized his mentoring style and his role,

123

even at an early age. Jiminy fights the darker forces and influences. He is a moral compass in the story. As an adult, I realized I like the character design, voice, and style as well. I have become an avid collector of all Jiminy memorabilia, and one of my prized posses- sions is a signed lithograph from the original voice of Jiminy Cricket, Eddie Carroll. This movie was originally released in 1940, and I think perfectly illustrates the magic and vision of Walt Dis- ney. The messages are timeless. The emotions are authentic. There is suspense and action. The artistry is beautiful. The story makes you laugh, cry, catch your breath, and smile. It also made me learn.

For me, Jiminy represents a tangible reminder to listen to your conscience and believe in yourself. We all have an inner voice that can work with you or against you. I always talk about yearn- ing for unconditional love; well, the reality is that you first have to love yourself unconditionally. You have to accept the complete you . . . internally and externally. It is obvious by now that most of my life was a yawning chasm of insecurities and I was con- stantly trying to fill some perceived voids. The journey to self- acceptance, and ultimately, self-love, has not been easy and takes a daily discipline. I can say that it does get easier as you age. With age, comes wisdom, or something like that. I hope that you find the calming peace of self-acceptance early in life, as I wasted too much time and money in therapy to be much of a role model for anyone. Negative self-talk holds back so much in your life. You find yourself constantly editing your thoughts and fighting against the harshness of your inner critic. For me, it is years of internal and external bullying that I battle against constantly.

Finally, after years of work and support, I feel in control of the dialogue. At least I understand the triggers and the signs more effectively. That has allowed me to grow.

To be a successful leader, you have to exercise and employ all of the tools available to you. Some of these tools are innate and part of your DNA, but many of these tools can be learned, nurtured, groomed, and earned over time. As I stated earlier, you should never really be done learning and growing, so your toolkit should constantly evolve.

My wonderful executive coach at Disney, David Oldfield, wrote a book called *Winnowing*. He coached me on separating the good learnings from the bad learnings, like separating the wheat from the chaff. His guidance was focused on my personal development as much as my professional growth and success. I am so grateful for that support and those insights. The winnowing concept is about your leadership toolkit, constantly evaluating what are important tools and skills to keep in your tool belt, and what you can let go of in order to grow.

My leadership success is a hard-earned combination of experience, intuition, and data. I believe in fact-based decision making, but I also believe you have to "trust your gut" and your inner voice (for me Mr. Cricket) to fully address obstacles, new inputs, and opportunities. This constant balancing act of instinct versus facts is a skill that is learned and developed over time. It needs to be exercised and you need to make some mistakes, which is fine as long as you are learning and failing forward. One of the best things about my tenure at Disney was its commitment to continuing executive education. We had annual curriculums to complete, and I did many in-person on online courses as part of my role at Disney.

One major area of education for me was truly understanding my moral and ethical core and my "do not cross" lines.

I was raised spiritually and with a strong sense of right and wrong, at least as defined by my parents. The Golden Rule, Fieldings Do Not Lie, living with gratitude, and giving back are the foundations for my moral compass. I sometimes wonder if I had too strong of a compass, which I know sounds odd. It could be almost debilitating for me if I saw something unjust or unfair according to my standards. It would make me angry, frustrated, and very judgmental. I guess I was keenly aware of the socioeconomic and demographic disparities in the world, and maybe as a member of a marginalized community, I was more sensitive? I am not really sure, but it caused and still causes me some grief. I watched other people "play the game" and I would get superior and indignant: "I would never be that political! I want to be recognized and rewarded for my hard work and honesty." I was always keeping score. Ironically, I am very good at spotting the politics and monitoring the "palace intrigue." I think I got the skill from my Dad and from working in Hollywood. It is almost a parlor game of sorts. I know this all sounds judgmental, and I am not saying I am always right and fair; it is just a major focus area for me.

At times, I struggled in corporate America as there were moments where I felt my beliefs were subjugated or compromised to the company's direction and goals. This was particularly troublesome for me working in LA/Hollywood and the big studios. With large media companies come large egos and almost built-in conflicts and tensions between work groups. The same could be said of large retail. The silos and artificial walls in most of the companies I worked at felt very real and very physical, like obstacles in a precarious scavenger hunt.

My conscience worked full-time talking to me while I worked at corporate HQ of the Gap in San Francisco. One example of this internal dialogue was with a trainee who was assigned to my merchandising office as part of his onboarding period. He came with an excellent résumé and some experience, and he presented as smart, eager to learn, and hard working. Within a week, I realized he was lazy and believed his background, connections, and family ties were more important than actually working and learning the role. He had attended all the "right" schools since kindergarten. His family was in social clubs with several members of the executive team. He was connected to the son of the CEO through several social circles. I worked with him to teach him the fundamentals of being a solid and successful merchant, but he was not focused on that. He simply wanted to be "placed" and promoted out of the trainee program so he could begin his career climb. I gave him honest and direct feedback, kept my boss in the loop, and communicated his strengths and developmental opportunities to HR and the training group lead.

One day, I was called into my boss's office to be told that this trainee was being promoted two levels to an associate merchandise manager and would be leaving the training program early to launch a new department in paper and stationery. I was stunned. He was not close to being ready. The new product category did not make sense to me. At that time, Gap was THE destination and we used to joke that we could sell almost anything. But paper and journals? It seemed to be a stretch.

I left the office, found the trainee, congratulated him, and then asked how this had transpired without my knowledge. He basically admitted he had worked around me, pitched a secret project directly to the CEO, and somehow developed a full proposal while I was traveling overseas and he was supposed to cover our area needs.

On the surface, I remained remarkably calm, but underneath I was seething. I felt manipulated and betrayed. I also felt that because he was a straight, handsome, white, and connected male he was receiving preferential treatment, and that violated all of my ethical filters. It also triggered my insecurities and perceived systemic inequities. To be honest, I handled it horribly, and that episode turned into a big learning lesson for me. I basically froze him out. I did nothing to help him transition to his new role or ensure his success. I basically felt he had made his bed, and now he had to lie in it. He struggled and I watched that with a certain amount of glee; the German word is *schadenfreude*! I moved on and focused on my team and my next trainee.

Incidentally, the area he launched failed and he left the company 18 months later. I never said "I told you so" to anyone, but I could not help thinking that the fates have an interesting way of handling situations. This is not a great example of leadership, however, and I do wish I had handled the situation differently.

Another example, or moment of truth, of when I had to trust my intuition to make a decision was my freshman year at Indiana University. I had convinced my Dad that attending an out-of-state school, with more cost and debt, was worth the investment due to its world-class business school. At that time, you had to complete a set of courses in your first two years and achieve a 3.0 GPA to enter the business school as a junior. That happy coincidence and plan changed the course of my collegiate studies. I was focused on business school and hitting the required grades and classes, but I did not enjoy the classes. In truth, I did not like them at all. I struggled through calculus; in fact, I had to take it twice! Statistics, computer programming, accounting . . . I was bored and distracted. My art and music classes, history, and political science electives, however, were stimulating and eye-opening. I felt I was seeing the world through different eyes. I was engaging in debates and critical discussions. I was problem solving. I was writing papers and defending my positions and views. I was becoming a global citizen and could feel my growth and changing perspective. I looked forward to my "general education" courses much more than my core business classes.

At the end of my freshman year, during my second semester, I received three *A*s, one *B*, and a *D* in calculus. I was mortified. A *D* in calculus would not meet the requirement for the business school admission, so I would have to stay for summer school and repeat the class. You can imagine that phone call home. My Dad was livid. I had wasted time and hard-earned money and now would not work enough in the summer to save for the upcoming year. Nevertheless, he agreed I really had no choice, and so I moved into my sophomore housing early and began an intensive six-week course in calculus, and I also took accounting to get ahead. The repetitive, daily nature of summer session forced calculus into my head, and I logged a *B*+.

Something else happened that summer. I decided that I wanted to major in political science; I was going to be a liberal arts student. This required another intense telephone conversation with my Dad. I was amazed he actually listened and remained calm. By the end of the conversation, I had agreed to major in political science, but pursue an outside field in business administration through the Honors College individualized major program. In this way, I was following my instinct for the value of a liberal arts education combined with the facts and realities of an IU business school emphasis. That decision as a 19-year-old changed the trajectory of my life and my career. It was the first major adult decision I made where I realize, with hindsight, I made by listening to my "Jiminy" and balancing that voice with educated research.

I dove into my liberal arts education and all that a Big Ten campus has to offer in the arts and the humanities. I loved my major in political science and all of the coursework, so much in fact, that in my senior year I was an undergraduate teaching assistant to Dr. James Christoph. Dr. Christoph was my favorite professor, and he asked me to assist him and his graduate assistant with a freshman-level course, Introduction to Comparative Politics (Y107). I had returned from my semester abroad in Copenhagen, Denmark (the DIS program), and had a global and fresh perspective on geopolitics and socioeconomics. I had a wonderful experience in Denmark learning about the Scandinavian culture, people, and social welfare system. I was blessed with an amazing host family who never spoke a word of English to me for six months. I came back to IU full of personal and academic growth, and was convinced I wanted to be an international lawyer or a college professor. My senior year journey had a few more wonderful examples of balancing my head, heart, and gut instinct. These were learnings my younger self needed!

After my time in Copenhagen, I returned to Bloomington in fall 1986 full of new ideas, new realizations, and new personal growth. I had turned 21 years old in Denmark and fully explored the European Continent, Scandinavia, and the nightlife scene in Copenhagen. I had expanded my mindset and perspective in the classroom through interacting with my Danish family and exploring my sexuality and sexual identity. I felt free in Denmark, probably for the first time in my life. I seriously considered extending my stay there, but the weight of financial debt and family expectations brought me home. After a summer of mononucleosis and lack of work, I returned to campus with energy and the need to work to stave off more debt. My senior year was demanding academically due to my two majors, and I felt lonely as many of my best friends had graduated while I was overseas. I was basically in class, studying, or at work. I was also preparing for the LSAT exam, as I was convinced that law school was my next step. I also was leading twice-a-week discussion sessions with freshmen students in Y107, Introduction to Comparative Politics.

Personally, I fell back into my closeted existence and was leading a fully double personal life. Throughout senior year, I dated a man and a woman. The man knew about my situation; the woman did not, for which I still feel so much guilt. My one friend on campus who knew what was going on called my social life "the revolving door." I was young, naïve, a little arrogant, and sure that I was bisexual. I truly cared for the woman, even loved her. I could see myself marrying her and having children, and living in a house with a white picket fence—the complete picture of Midwestern suburban bliss. We would belong to all the right clubs, have smart and charming kids, and two sweet dogs. The only problem was I would be living a lie. When I was with the man I was dating, I was happier, lighter, freer, and more authentically me. I felt emotions and passion I had never experienced before. He pushed me to embrace my truth. I pushed back and kept our relationship on the down low and private. As senior year progressed, it became clear that financing law school would be an issue for me. In addition, I was really drawn to a life in academia. Also, people were advising me to go out in the real world and work for a few years before any type of graduate school.

I had a life-changing/moment of truth meeting with Dr. Christoph. I told him I wanted to get a masters and PhD in political science and I wanted him to be my advisor and mentor. I will never forget his brutal honesty and assessment of me and the situation. He told me I did not love the research requirements of advanced degrees in political science. He said I loved the "teaching" part . . . the in-classroom discussions and interactions with the students. He told me he was worried I would end up as the most popular civics teacher or world politics teacher at some random high school in the Midwest. I would be effective, but I would never be fulfilled and the pay would always be an issue. It was so blunt, it shocked me almost like a slap in the face. He encouraged me to pursue law school or a career in international business instead.

I was devastated, but I knew he was right. But law school was not a viable financial option immediately, so I pursued the interview process through the business school. Another perfect example of listening to my instincts and acknowledging the facts. That one conversation set off chain reactions for the next 35 years that I still experience. When Dr. Christoph passed, I wrote a letter to his widow and children. I wanted them to know how grateful I was for his brilliance, his wisdom, his compassion, and his direction. He saw something in me I had not yet realized myself. He set me on my career course. Another vivid example of mentorship in my life.

The story of my personal balancing act of feelings and facts my senior year is another painful, yet supremely important, moment of truth in my life. As I approached graduation in spring 1987, I had successfully managed the duality of my life, or so I thought. Both of my "partners" were pushing me for my plans post-graduation and their part in those plans. Rather than stepping up and confronting my truth, I strung them both along. I was blessed with multiple job offers for retail training programs in a variety of interesting cities like Chicago, Atlanta, New Orleans, Miami, and Minneapolis. The female partner had three cities in common with my list and was leaning toward her Atlanta opportunity. The male partner overlapped only in New Orleans and had accepted that opportunity. He was pushing me to accept my New Orleans opportunity so we could move together and start a life as an open couple in a very friendly city. I could not handle that. I also did not think it was my best job offer, but the reality was I was ill prepared to live the life he was designing for us. To his credit, he dumped me. I was destroyed and I deserved it.

In the meantime, I focused on my Minneapolis opportunity. Not only was it the best training program and team, but also the woman was planning on moving to Atlanta. In my devious, insecure, and immature mind, this meant we could break up by using the excuse of a long-distance relationship and needing to focus on the early phases of our careers. One week before our decision deadline, she asked me to come to a dinner at her house and to write the name of the job and city I was accepting and place it in a sealed envelope. She was going to do the same, and we agreed to abide by whatever was written on the cards, regardless of what that meant to our relationship. I was a nervous wreck as I drove to the dinner, but I did see this as a weak man's escape plan and a chance to move to a new city and write a new chapter alone. I was slowly coming to understand myself and felt I needed to close this chapter. We did not wait to eat. We instantly ripped open the envelopes and my heart sank. We had both written Minneapolis.

I put on a brave face and faked my way through graduation and the move to the Twin Cities. The saving grace was her very conservative family, which meant we had separate apartments and very different work schedules. This was an era of no cell phones, texts, emails. It was about answering machines and random messages on work phones. I was able to use the training program demands as an excuse constantly to avoid her. The sad truth is that I withdrew, became an asshole, and allowed the relationship to atrophy. All due to my weakness and inability to own and speak the truth. I regret this episode and story completely. No one deserves that type of treatment, and I carry the guilt with me to this day. I was able to keep tabs on her and I know she has built a wonderful family and career, but I wish I could have been man enough to speak the facts. My conscience, my Jiminy, my self-talk was horrible during the early months of summer 1987. I was very depressed, very scared, and very insecure. The work was going great, though, and I was falling in love with retail and the opportunities in that industry.

My final story in this learning is about my journey to self-acceptance and living with pride. It is also about my journey to leadership with pride and living authentically. It is a wonderful example of using my instinct and balancing those insights with facts and realities. Leadership is a process and a privilege; it is not a right or a position.

RuPaul says, "If you cannot love yourself, how in the hell are you going to love someone else," and "Can I get an AMEN." All I can say is "AMEN!"

I spent most of my adolescence and young adulthood loathing myself. I felt broken, deviant, and less than others. I was confused, scared, hurt, and nervous all the time. For a long time, I just wanted to change. In addition to my homosexuality, I dealt with all the other so-called normal teen issues like body image, acne, puberty and constant horniness, and parental angst. I was obsessed with what other people thought of me and was constantly searching for external validation. Growing up is hard! It is even harder when you continually talk negatively to yourself and have those negative thoughts consistently reinforced by others. The Jiminy/Conscience self-talk had to work overtime to overcome the cacophony of negativity, judgment, and outright self-destructive tendencies. I am here to tell you, however, that it does get better, and you can come out on the other side . . . as a secure, successful, somewhat calm, and mature person who actually enjoys themselves and their total identity.

Over the years of my adulthood, I did a lot of therapy. I did a lot of group work. I did a lot of reading. I did a lot of research. That is the fact-based side of my brain. I had to convince myself, before convincing others, that I was made this way. I had to understand the science and the theories. I devoured the Kinsey Institute work. (Ironically, this research was done at Indiana University by Dr. Alfred Kinsey and his associates and supported and protected by Chancellor Herman B. Wells, a hero at my alma mater.) This work was the journey to self-acceptance, and ultimately, to self-love.

As I grew and matured and blossomed, I was able to have calm and rational conversations with important people in my life who struggled with my reality and story. I have told my story to many different people and groups. It always is the same. My sexual orientation is not a choice. I am not a deviant. I do not recruit new members of the club. I was meant to be this way. There are others like me. Being gay does not make me weaker, dumber, more emotional, or less capable of leading. In fact,

I believe my path and my truth make me special. I am one of a kind. I am living the life I was meant to live. Sure, I am a little bruised. I am getting thicker-skinned every day. My hair is thinning. I have new aches every morning. But, I love my life. I love me. Jiminy and the facts are in harmony. GRATITUDE! Remember this learning as you progress in your life and career. You, too, have an intuition and inner voice that you need to actively engage with on a regular basis. Trust me, you are wiser and smarter than you believe.

8 | Building High-Performing Teams and Cultures of Excellence

I have always been team-, group-, and club-oriented. I was a competitive swimmer when I was younger, and I enjoyed the individual races and challenges, but the team relays and results were always more fun for me. Any of the multiple personality, leadership, or skills assessment work I have done always points me toward leadership roles and communal work groups and industries. While most people view me as an extrovert and talkative leader, I have many introverted needs and tendencies. Sometimes, especially after an intense period of work or stress, my body will just shut down and I will rest and sleep for an entire weekend. I love my alone time. I am constantly thinking and can debate anything from several angles and perspectives. Over the years, I have learned what works for me and my needs, but I have also learned to assess what a team needs to be engaged and successful. I do feel that I have some innate skills and my personality is suited to leadership roles, but I also believe you can learn to be a more effective leader.

As I hit the later stages of my career, I am very proud of my reputation as a team and culture builder. I am always committed to recruiting, developing, and retaining diverse and talented individuals to form a dynamic and innovative team. Learning #8 is probably the most business-focused learning, but these insights were formed by my personality, approach to leadership, and failing forward from mistakes. I also have been blessed to work for some extraordinary and visionary leaders, and I have harvested wisdom from all of them. The reality is that these insights work for many situations in your life, including your family, social groups and clubs, and community. I hope you find some valuable tools or insights from my stories. I believe in the importance of transparent and collaboration relationships within your work group and with the teams you support. I was successful in large and matrixed corporations simply because I was committed to building relationships at all levels of the organization. I managed up, down, and sideways. I worked hard to know people's names and stories, and I truly believe that every intern, assistant, or group president is of equal importance to the team and should be treated accordingly. Any time I entered a new role or company, I would engage in a series of "meet and greets" and engage my active listening skills. It is so important and will pay off many times over, if you take the time to build relationships.

I believe you need to create environments where people understand their role and how their work performance will help the team achieve its goals. I firmly believe in qualitative and quantitative goals and breaking down those goals into small, digestible pieces that your team can truly own and influence. If the goals are too lofty or too esoteric or perceived as too unattainable, you are dead in the water from day one. For me, it starts with a three- to five-year strategic plan process that is inclusive, transparent, and collaboratively developed. This can mean it takes more time to finish, but the results and the buy-in are priceless. I believe that good ideas can come from anywhere and that two heads are better than one. I do not believe in levels of authority deciding the total vision. I do feel, however, that you earn your way into the strategic vision exercises with time and performance, but you have to be willing to be execution-oriented at times in your career. If you use your active listening skills and involve as many voices as possible, you will be surprised what you will learn. Many of our best business strategies and innovative ideas came out of brainstorming sessions or sharing seemingly random insights in a group meeting.

I personally am challenged by the realities of our work locations and situation now (post-pandemic). I have tried every video conference and whiteboard tool out there and have yet to find an acceptable alternative to in-person sessions. I sometimes feel so old-school, like I am not willing to work with the admittedly amazing technological advances available to us now. I just love the feeling of collaboration and seeing someone unexpected deliver an extraordinary idea. It is an almost electric feeling. People who work with me will tell you that when the hairs stand up on my arms when I hear something interesting, that is a good sign! I also worry about missing the innovation opportunities that happen spontaneously in the hallways, the elevators, during lunch breaks, and in the coffee room. I have always had an "open-door policy," and it is meant to allow free flow of conversations and ideas. Of course, I employed amazing gatekeepers, and there were and are times I need to work behind closed doors, but I try to keep that to a minimum. Now, I embrace that, by opening up your mind to this new hybrid way of working and not being bound by geography, you are opening your access to true talent.

I have always worked very hard on getting a team into proper "flying formation." Others would say things "all rowing in the same direction" or "a guiding North Star," but it all means the same thing. Involve everyone, actively listen, encourage dialog and debate, and watch what happens. At Disney Store, we were solving complex and puzzling challenges. I believed we had the right organization structure, the right talent, and the right mission and vision, we were just missing something special, the "pixie dust." I realized that this was culture. You cannot flip a switch and say now we have culture. You have to be patient and nudge progress along, especially with geographically dispersed teams. You also need to acknowledge and embrace language and cultural differences around the world. You need to learn how to navigate appropriately in Japan, Italy, France, and so on . . . and still maintain adherence to the core mission and vision. A working knowledge of world history and current political science and economics is also an excellent skill to have in your toolkit.

As a post-pandemic leader, I advise my clients and my own company to embrace the realities of today's workforce and competition for talent. I believe we must embrace a hybrid and flexible work policy, especially when it comes to mandatory office time. I truly believe the employees are fully in charge now, and employers need to adapt to attract and retain the best and the brightest. I do not think we will ever return to five days a week in an office setting, or even to a majority of days in an office. I have had to learn new techniques and skills to navigate this new world. Most of my career, I have built teams using physical co-location and communication events in person. Now, most of my work is virtual and remote. I still believe it is important to pull your team together for key work events or strategy sessions, but as the leader, you must create and craft these opportunities to maximize the in-person times. The worst you can do is mandate that people come into an office and they spend their entire day in virtual meetings in some type of phone booth.

I also feel this hybrid approach allows an employer to fully embrace diversity in hiring, as you expand the pool of talent looking outside a traditional office radius. Younger employees now (for my purposes defined as under 30) have a very different set of filters for choosing employers than my generation employed. Compensation is always a determining factor, but the younger employees now rank flexibility, corporate values, and employee respect higher than medical benefits and a 401(k) plan. They are also very conscious of the communities they are allowed to live in based on their employer choice. My niece, who recently graduated magna cum laude from the University of Arizona ("guncle" brag!), chose her first company because she could live in the Pacific Northwest and that region of the country aligned with her political and societal beliefs.

For an employer competing for talent in this environment, we must adapt to these new realities. It is like I always say in media, the consumer is in charge of programming their content now. In a similar fashion, talented employees are in charge of the job search and choice, and we have to show them how we are going to enable their personal and professional needs and growth. As a leader, you must commit to communication, mentorship, and building culture with this new type of work life. As a Darwin follower, I say we must adapt or wither away. If we do not figure this out, our competitors will.

One technique I used at Disney Store to build culture and team-work was called the "4 Cs": Creativity, Collaboration, Communication, and Community. I worked hard on this list and made sure they translated into numerous languages and cultures seamlessly and accurately. For a year, I trained and communicated repeatedly on the 4 Cs. I had them made into posters, note cards, and stickers. I ended every email with them. I used humor and facts to make them stick. I used to say to any group I was with, "You are all creatives; it is not just the product developers or character artists or marketers, and I encourage all of you to exercise your creative muscles. If you are in finance or accounting, however, you need to still color within the lines, as your work is keeping me honest!" I wanted these words to come to life in our work environment, in our stores, our e-commerce operations, and our warehouses. As our culture and team grew and came together at Disney Store, we added a fifth C "Celebration," which was a way to pause, appreciate, and recognize all types and sizes of achievements.

Out of this work, I came to fully engage with the concept of GLOCAL, global and local smashed together. This meant blending the best of both worlds and allowing for local execution and ownership. I came to understand how important it was to set global vision and standards, but to allow for local implementation and execution with small, but important changes that worked in that particular community. We created recognition awards in the stores and our home office to celebrate our global Disney Store Brand Ambassadors.

Understand, I knew I had to create jobs that felt bigger than just punching a clock. I knew there was a war for talent, and I needed to hold on to the team. I also believed and still believe that it is not just about the pay or the benefits or the bonuses. In fact, it is about how you feel about where you work. How you are appreciated. The people you work with. Feeling like you are contributing to something that matters. It was about participating fully and authentically and being engaged. From that, I fully believe, comes performance that will exceed any goals. This philosophy is why I learned the choreography to "We Are All in This Together" from *High School Musical* and dressed up like a Troll for a sales meeting in Las Vegas where I presented in costume with Justin Timberlake, or why I wrote personal birthday and thank you cards regularly. I do it because I truly love my job, and I want people to understand they are valued.

I am convinced that I over-index in this area based on my queerness and my lifelong feeling of not fitting in somewhere. I never want anyone on our team to feel less than someone else, or that their ideas are unimportant or less relevant than another person's opinion or ideas. My insecurities and inferiority complex probably make me much more sensitive in this area. The kind of work I do and the industries I work in are people-driven and ideas-driven. The highest capital investment is in human resources, and I believe team engagement and involvement are the keys to successful team building and performance. Commitment to a culture of excellence and engagement is not optional, it is imperative. I sometime wonder, and I have no empirical data or research to prove it, if in this area my queerness is actually a competitive advantage? Maybe it is my "superpower"? I am not bragging or saying I am better than my peers, but I do realize I have been able to lead more effectively once I fully embraced my authentic self and used every piece of me to its potential. I am at my best when I "let go" and just use all of me to be fully present in a situation or in leading a team. It is the first time in my life I have ever considered my homosexuality to be an advantage or a gift, and that is huge progress.

One story I love to share as an example of my leadership philosophy was a team-building event I hosted in Madrid, Spain, in 2007 when I was the head of global retail sales and marketing for Disney Consumer Products. It is honestly one of my favorite memories and stories from my time in this role. I am also very aware that it was a unique moment in time, when our business was on fire, our team was performing at a high level, and I had a supportive leader who enabled this type of event.

Our team was geographically dispersed and used to communicating virtually via email and conference calls. Some of us gathered at licensing fairs and other trade events, but we had never gathered our entire team in one place for team building, strategic planning, and individual skills development. It was also an opportunity for social engagement and celebrating team success. I had incredible planning partners in Joanne, John, and Jim and we worked on the logistics and agenda for over six months.

We chose to host in Madrid due to its major airport accessibility, space availability, cost, and market importance. We built a comprehensive agenda and chose a fascinating host hotel called the Hotel Puerta America. We took over the entire hotel with over 200 people in attendance. What I loved was that each floor had been designed by a famous interior designer or architect, including Norman Foster, Zaha Hadid, Jean Nouvel, and other global icons. Each floor was so custom and distinct; it was a great message on innovation and design for our team to embrace. It was also a kind of icebreaker for people to talk about the design elements of their floor and room.

One of the highlights of the event was a scavenger hunt we designed for teams of four that took the groups all over Madrid, learning local history, culture, gastronomy, and Disney trivia. It culminated in a sumptuous banquet of Spanish delicacies and classic dishes. It was amazing to watch a friendly, yet competitive, game bring a global team together—overcoming any language or cultural differences and uniting people who work on common goals and have a common short-term focus. We did ensure each team had a Spanish speaker to insure safety and completion!

On the opening morning of the conference, I shocked the attendees by delivering my entire 15-minute welcome comments in Spanish. I had been studying Spanish quietly through Berlitz for six months and worked so hard with my tutor to set the tone for the meeting. I wanted to show the team that we did not have a USA bias, that we were truly a global team, that communication in all languages and all cultures were valued. I will never forget the look on people's faces as I began and continued the entire speech in my best Spanish I could muster, stopping to quickly translate intermittently for the English-speaking crowd. I was very proud of my efforts and the comments I received from the team, especially the native Spanish speakers in attendance. I was grateful to my Venezuelan Berlitz tutor who gave me such great training and a clean accent! Every time I meet up with the one of the attendees, regardless of how long it has been and where they work now, I always hear how important this event was to them at the time. It created treasured memories and lasting bonds, and may have been the best group event I have ever created or attended.

Incidentally (or maybe not), our performance for the two years immediately following the meeting exceeded all goals and expectations. The investment in that event paid off tenfold and had positive lasting impact. I am confident that the investment in bringing everyone together paid off in our results for many years and that skills and connections made in Madrid stand the test of time.

★ ★ ★

I have been exposed to many different kinds of leaders and style of leadership over my career and in my various nonprofit board roles. I try to learn something from all of them and thought I would share some of my favorite learnings from some of the leaders I have respected the most in my career.

Jeffrey Katzenberg is a true Hollywood legend. His career and his commitment to community is legendary. Before I worked for him, I had heard all of the rumors and stories about his leadership and communication style. He was known for his three breakfast meetings in a row, and the same for lunches. I can confirm that his work ethic and energy level were intimidating in their intensity, but also very inspiring. I had many meetings with him over breakfast in all three time slots. They always started and ended on time, always had an agenda, and I always walked away having learned something and with a new challenge. There was also a quote attributed to Jeffery that goes something like "If you are late for work on Saturday, do not come in on Sunday." I believe that was from early in his career when he was tapped to lead Disney Animation. Personally, I think I worked for the more mellow and wise Mr. Katzenberg. Yes, you received messages all the time. Yes, your phone would ring and you would hear his amazing assistant say, "I have Jeffery for you," but she also asked, "Was it a good time?" You had the choice to take or return the call, and it did not feel career limiting to choose a later option. The other leaders whom Jeffrey surrounded himself with, like Ann Daly and Michael Francis, were a critical part of his success and leadership philosophy. Talent attracts talent.

What I learned from Jeffrey was his passionate commitment to creativity and quality. His attention to detail is simply world-class and awe-inspiring. I also admired his amazing network of creative talents and his ability to contact anyone on a moment's notice for important needs and decisions. Creative talent loved working with him, and he supported and respected the best and brightest. Jeffrey is also an idea fountain; he was constantly ideating new approaches and products in our space. He was willing to drop everything and attend important license or retail meetings at a moment's notice. He was an incredible asset throughout our work on the *Trolls* movie and the accompanying product and promotions activity. Due to his leadership and vision, we were able to take over the famed Macy's red shopping bag façade and convert it to a Trolls shopping bag three stories high! We were also able to fully leverage the promotional opportunities with the support of Anna Kendrick and Justin Timberlake. Their acting and vocal supremacy made so many retailer and licensee relationships possible globally. Due to Jeffrey's vision, relationships, and personal requests, we were able to secure the largest merchandising program in Dreamworks history.

Jeffrey's incredible commitment to philanthropy and giving back to his community was also very educational for me. His entire family serves as role models for making a difference and using their talent and treasure to create positive change in the world. I was especially touched by their personal support for GLSEN and for the Motion Pictures and Television Academy retirement home and community. Intelligence, compassion, drive, and vision are what I took away from the privilege of working with him. He built incredible teams and led them with intensity and loyalty, but you also felt supported to take risks creatively and try something new.

Due to Jeffrey's support and introduction, I was able to secure a meeting with Stacey Snider, who would become my last "corporate" boss and a leader I came to admire greatly. When we met, Stacey had recently been named chairperson of the 20th Century Fox Movie business, and after the Dreamworks merger with Comcast NBCUniversal, I had become available again. I planned to meet her for lunch to discuss consulting for six months to a year to establish my independent advisory business, Intersected Stories. I was very honored and excited to meet her as she had produced a very important movie called *Philadelphia* starring Tom Hanks and Denzel Washington, and had worked with Steven Spielberg for years. She was also a kind of unicorn in Hollywood, as she was a female head of a major movie studio.

I did my homework and approached the lunch with an eager and open mind. I intended to pitch Stacey on a one-year advisory role helping her build out her consumer products and experiences group. As the lunch progressed, it became clear that Stacey wanted a permanent solution. She connected me to Peter Rice, the head of television, and told me she wanted a leader who could support both the film and television groups. After a few weeks and a series of interviews with some amazing people, including Dana Walden, Gary Newman, and John Landgraf, I realized that I really wanted this role. Everyone I met was more talented, visionary, and supportive than the person before them. They also admitted they had never been great at consumer products or experiences and wanted a new direction and path. They were committed to success in our space and industry. I was now officially motivated to land a permanent role, and I moved to build the team and gain Stacey's support for my vision and structure.

This is what I learned from her in this process. Throughout our negotiations and my onboarding and first 90 days, she remained focused, supportive, inquisitive, and committed to our team's success. In addition, she went out of her way to learn about me as a person and my family life. She was never intrusive, never prying . . . she authentically was interested in getting to know me. Every meeting with her always started with 5–10 minutes of updates on our lives outside of the office. She shared her family updates, actively listened to mine, and remembered everything we had ever discussed. I realized this was her authentic leadership and communication style, and how she built high-performing and loyal teams of leaders. She respected my talents and my diversity, and encouraged me to be a vocal and visible leader on her team. She never asked me to wait for the right time, or to earn my spot at the table, which was very unusual in Hollywood.

These skills and traits became critical during the transition period when Disney was buying Fox. Stacey was always accessible. She was always transparent and honest in her communications. She shared her frustrations and vulnerability openly throughout the tense moments, especially as the time dragged on. She earned our trust and support because she felt like one of us. Like us, she was going through a long and arduous corporate merger that she could not control. Throughout the many months, she always made time to talk to me about what my plans were post-merger and our "exit date." She was kind, empathetic, and wise. I started to wonder if this was how strong women managed, but I do not want to attribute her skills to her gender. I do not want to diminish her by talking about how she navigated in a misogynistic and patriarchal old-boy's system. Instead, I choose to celebrate and elevate her talent and live in gratitude that I got to work with her and for her. She taught me new skills and made me appreciate her leadership style immensely. That transitional period was a trying time for all of us, but working with and for Stacey made it bearable.

I have had the pleasure of working with and for other strong women in my career as well, particularly in the last few years. I want to share these stories as examples of diverse leadership styles and experiences, to explain what I have taken away from my time with them.

The first story is about Sofia Vergara, who at times has been the highest paid actress in Hollywood. Of course, she earned good money from her incredible run as Gloria on *Modern Family*, but the truth is her vast earnings are from her intelligent and visionary entrepreneurial side. Along with her business partner and friend, Luis Balaguer, Sofia has built a differentiated and impressive array of business ventures. Luis and Sofia engaged my team at Then What to work with them on a five-year brand plan for Team Sofia, which coincided with the end new episodes of *Modern Family*.

As we worked with her, I learned so many interesting facts and stories about her as an actress, a woman, a mother, and a business owner. I cannot share all of them due to the confidential nature of our work for her, but I can share a few anecdotes to illustrate my admiration. From a very young age, Sofia was one of the most beautiful and successful talents in the Spanish-speaking world. She was a very important part of the success of Univision and Telemundo, and relocated to Miami from her native Colombia as a young, newly divorced mother. Rather than rest on her beauty and talent, she organized and energized her peers into an important movement and voice in Latin entertainment. Again, I cannot divulge the entire story, as it is hers to tell, but out of this movement grew her company Latin World Entertainment. To this day, Latin WE is one of the largest and most important management agencies and producers in the industry. Luis Balaguer, her long-time business partner and friend, also taught me about creative collaboration and strategic business planning. They are wonderful examples of right-brain and left-brain synergy in respectful partnerships.

In addition, Sofia has always had a vision and passion for fashion, design, hospitality, and home decor. Not content to "label slap" her name and likeness on a variety of disparate promotions, she instead committed to building brands, leveraging her intellect and reach. As her company built over time, she surrounded herself with bright and loyal talented people, and built her own community and work family. She also wisely utilized her natural family's talents and assets as well. I could have written about Sofia and Luis in the chosen family section of this book as well, but my real learnings are more suited for this section. Sofia's Latin WE and her entire approach to life are incredible examples of how to build culture, energy, and high-performing teams.

As we worked on her brand plan, we began pushing ourselves to new insights and heights of performance simply because we wanted to meet or exceed her team's expectations. Presenting to her, debating with her, and learning from her are highlights in the advisory stages of my career. I feel very lucky to have spent time with her, Luis, and their entire team.

The next strong leader I have learned from is my friend, peer, and current chairman at Archer Gray, Amy Nauiokas. I first met Amy when we served together on the Make-A-Wish Foundation International Board of Directors. At our first meeting, I was drawn to her intelligence, charm, and laser focus. As we began to work together, I learned her fascinating personal story, which I am pushing her to write in her own book someday. Suffice to say, when they made Amy, they threw away the mold. Amy is a change agent and a glass ceiling breaker. She is one of the "firsts" in so many areas, including Wall Street and London financial firms. She is also an incredible Mom, friend, daughter, sister, confidante, and role model. She is passionately committed to supporting change in systems that have historically been rigged against underrepresented communities and voices. She has founded many companies and invested in many others, but her greatest achievements in business are the founding of Anthemis and Archer Gray.

Anthemis is a venture capital fund that invests wisely in businesses globally, mainly in the financial tech space and in companies founded by nontraditional visionaries. Archer Gray, where I am now a partner, is an independent media company committed to quality storytelling in all formats, building businesses, and amplifying voices from underserved communities. Amy has always had a vision on how these two companies would intersect to help her positively impact the world. She is consistent and insistent that we use our power and voices to correct historical systemic inequities.

Amy is brilliant, and occasionally, it takes me some time to catch up to her vision, but when I do, I am always struck by the beauty and power of her goals. She makes me want to be better at my role. And she supports my lifelong desire to be ever growing and learning. I am excited to build our shared vision of the future with the entire Archer Gray team under her leadership and our new CEO, Vinay Singh. My role at Archer Gray allows me to stretch myself creatively and operationally, and I love the simple freedom of variety in my daily activities and meetings that this role brings to me. I also learn from Amy watching her navigate her roles as wife, mother, ex-wife, friend, daughter, and sister. She is a great role model.

Of course, I have to share my Disney leadership learnings in this chapter. I know I have already shared many insights from my almost 12-year tenure at the Mouse House, but I have to credit Andy Mooney and Bob Iger in this chapter with what they taught me as I worked and grew there. I am confident that my knowledge of and commitment to forming high-performing team cultures was honed at Disney. I saw versions of servant leadership and executive excellence everywhere. Disney invested in me through a variety of seminars, experiences, and meetings to learn new skills. I wish more companies would invest in personal and professional development opportunities at all levels.

And, as mentioned before, I was blessed with an incredible executive coach, David Oldfield. Disney Consumer Products Human Resources, led by Susan Garelli, also taught me the importance of tangible measurement of engagement and active listening. The annual Employee Culture Survey was not only a tool for measuring progress, but also a goal we were held accountable to in our performance reviews. It was as important to our leadership team under Andy as our financial performance, and we all passionately believed a motivated, focused, and engaged team would drive improved results.

Andy Mooney taught me how to focus on the team and simple building blocks to drive behavior and results. He had a way of distilling complex ideals and a large global business down to four building blocks that never changed under his leadership. I watched with awe and admiration as I traveled the world and saw the blocks translated in local languages, culture, and execution. Every speech, meeting, presentation, or hallway encounter with Andy had some element of the building blocks in the conversation. It was subtle, yet very effective, and you could watch it permeate every leader's presentations and messaging. It was a culture built out of constant reinforcement of mission, vision, and the building blocks to execution.

In this environment, I learned to improve my own communication techniques and how to build a subculture within this overall culture of performance. My emails, speeches, formal presentations, and simple meetings were all built off the four building blocks. "Java with Jim" was developed under this atmosphere as a way for me to connect directly with our team and to actively listen to their ideas and concerns. We randomly chose 12–15 people at varying intervals. They were invited to a conference room, handed a coffee mug and some snacks, and for one hour I would listen, learn, lead, and laugh. We promised confidentiality and a safe space, and no topics were off limits. I would always save 10 minutes at the end for rumors and myths, which allowed me to truly hear what the hallway chatter and concerns were. I still have two of those custom mugs we designed, and I cherish them. I have employed Java with Jim at all of my subsequent roles and companies. It all started with Andy's leadership style and vision.

Andy also taught me his philosophy of "Blaze and Graze." Andy was an incredible role model for working very hard during "work hours" and unplugging on weekends and vacations. His time out of the office with his family and friends was legendary and sacred. You could not contact him unless it was a life-threatening emergency! In this era of 24/7 connectivity and response immediacy expectations, Andy shines as the leader who knows how to turn off and trust others to do their jobs. He was always available if you truly needed him, but you felt supported and empowered to make the right decisions for your team and business without seeking his approval. He was the opposite of a micromanager, and I thrived under his direction and guidance. With hindsight, he was the perfect leader for that point in my career.

Robert (Bob) Iger is a globally recognized and legendary leader, communicator, and Fortune 50 CEO. All the accolades and stories are hard-earned, accurate, and crafted over time. I am blessed to have worked under his leadership for my entire tenure at Disney. It is interesting that half of my tenure was under Michael Eisner with Bob as his #2, and half was under the Bob Iger era, two equally impressive leaders who could not have been more different in their style and approach to the role. This is not a Disney leadership history, but the contrasts were striking and educational. Michael was all about competition and pitting the various business units against each other for talent, investment, and other resources. Mr. Iger employed a completely different leadership style and philosophy.

What I learned from Bob, among many things, was the art of communication and collaboration. Bob was always about the Disney brand first, and what the entire, disparate company would do to drive enterprise-wide results and how we could work well together to drive results and shareholder value. He was able to weave vision and team commitment that successfully made ABC, ESPN, and all the businesses under the Disney umbrella make sense. His visionary leadership style also created and oversaw the successful acquisitions of Pixar, Marvel, and Lucasfilm. All three of these companies had distinct and impressive cultures, yet Bob and his leadership team were able to successfully integrate them into the overall magic, with more than a splash or two of pixie dust. It was never easy, but it was clear we were all going to come together to create magical content and experiences for our guests around the world.

Bob believed in me, and when he shone his light on you, you worked harder and you believed more in yourself and your contribution. Without fail, Bob remembered people's names, where they worked, and some slice of personal anecdote that he would mention. I think that was what impressed me the most, Bob's ability to connect with people. It is probably why he was always mentioned as a possible candidate for public office. He made everyone feel special, respected, and part of the team. He was able to lead a massive global entertainment giant of over 180,000 and still make it feel personal and small. You understood your tangible impact to the overall success of the company, due to the culture he created. I have said it before, but I am forever grateful for that experience and that opportunity. Pixie dust is in my veins. Reading his book also inspired me to try to write my own and I hope he reads this passage at least!

One of my favorite and overused phrases at work is "So, what?" I used it so much, that my Fox team started to call it the "so what test." Let me explain. I dislike it when you are in meetings and people present data, research, or analysis and then do not present any insights or action plans. My response would always be, "So, what?"—meaning what does this mean and what are they suggesting we do as a team or business unit? People would approach me with a problem, and not offer any possible solutions, so I would ask, "So, what?", meaning what do you expect me to do with this information? Other times, I would learn that a particular person or team was feeling overworked or underappreciated and I would approach them and ask "So, what do you need?" I am sure you get the intent behind this phrase. I have no issue with identifying issues and obstacles, but I also want to hear possible solutions and work-arounds. I never claimed to have all of the good ideas and solutions. I encouraged our teams to present solutions, not just issues.

So, what did I learn from the leaders and stories I just shared with you?

From Andy, I learned TEAM FOCUS and BLAZE and GRAZE.

From Bob, I learned GLOBAL SCALE and MAKE WORK FEEL TANGIBLE and PERSONAL.

From Stacey, I learned COMPASSION and PASSION.

From Sofia, I learned to DIVERSIFY YOUR TALENT and FOCUS.

From Jeffrey, I learned DRIVE and WORK ETHIC.

From Amy, I learned to BE A SYSTEMIC CHANGE AGENT and use your platform for GOOD WORK.

From all of them, I learned to commit to QUALITY and EXCELLENCE, and to respect your personal life and balance.

I also want to revisit the Global Disney Store story as it is so relevant in this learning. That role and period of my life has shaped my leadership style more than any other experience. Along with the bosses I have mentioned, I would be remiss in not mentioning the global team I worked with from 2008 to 2012 and what they taught me as a person and leader. First, let me say again, it was an honor and privilege to work with this group. They pushed me to be better in ways I could have never imagined. Their passion, work ethic, imagination, and talent simply awed and humbled me. This is going to feel like a laundry list of names or a tedious acceptance speech at some awards ceremony, but each of these people touched me uniquely and helped me hone my skills.

Peter Collyer, our global head of Talent and People, was a constant truth teller and kept a temperature check on the team motivation and attitude. He never hesitated to tell me directly and frankly when I had done or said something wrong and when to pull back. Steve Finney, our COO, was an operational guru and had amazing attention to detail, which allowed me to be lofty and grand in my ambitions, as he grounded me in reality. Steve Gilbert was exactly the type of CFO I needed. Honest, forthright, incredibly detailed, and hyper-connected to Disney corporate finance. He had my back and figured out how to pay for the vision. Every idea fountain needs a detailed regulator to keep it on track.

The dynamic duo of Teresa Tideman and John Hobson owned the European regional vision and execution roles beautifully. They taught me so much about retail and culture in so many countries. I have so many fond memories of traveling in Europe with John and Teresa scouting locations for stores and remodels . . . planes, trains, automobiles, and shopping carts for our luggage. Exhausted most of the time, frustrated often, but so happy along the way.

Jon Endicott is the architect and imagineer you want running any project where practical magic and surprise are required. Robin Beuthin, who literally delivered her third child on the day of the first prototype opening, was a consummate creative and artistic leader. A Disney-trained and approved character artist (a rare bird!), she never wavered in pushing me to think bigger and differently about our brand. We moved Jonathan Storey from London to Los Angeles to lead our field operations team. His passionate commitment to the storytelling and magic of our brand created all the fantastic rituals and magical guidelines that made our stores do different. He even supervised the recording of our custom soundtrack in London's famous Abbey Road

Studios. This music, by the way, included our own title song from the Grammy and Tony award–winning team of Kristin Anderson-Lopez and Bobby Lopez. They are probably better known for writing "Let It Go" from the movie *Frozen*.

Finally, the trio of Ricky Phung, Scott Norville, and Sharon Zhen. Ricky did over 200 tours of the prototype space with me for a wide variety of audiences. I was so technologically inept I could not turn on the lighting without him. By the end, he could do the tour better than I could. Scott was my chief of staff, or "Jim whisperer." He did so much behind the scenes that I probably do not even know about. Most of his sentences began "What Jim really meant was . . . ," as he interpreted my frantic and crazy pace and way of speaking. Sharon was a consummate merchant who truly understood how to translate the vision into articles of clothing, another rare bird. The three of them moved to Shanghai as part of our time together prepping that market for the Disney Store entry to coincide with the Disneyland Park opening.

There are so many other names and stories I could share from Disney Store. If any of my former castmates are reading this and not seeing their name, please do not fret! You are all fondly remembered, and I am so grateful for your patience, guidance, wisdom, tenacity, and bravery. We did something amazing together. I know I will never have an opportunity like that again and I cherish those memories. Never forget the impact you made on kids and families around the world. To be honest, many of your postings on social media, especially LinkedIn, spurred me into writing this book. It is very hard for me to read all the goodbye messages as Disney Stores around the world are slowly closing. I follow each and every person's path and I am confident that wherever a former Disney Store castmate lands, that company is a winner for finding your talent. I cherish your stories and the mementos I have gathered over the years. You were all part of something very special and should have nothing but pride in what you created.

All of these people have helped craft the leader and person I am today in their own way. I believe in Keeping It Simple, but being a leader today is never easy. I have never seen so many challenges and roadblocks thrown in the paths of leaders. The global economy, geopolitical conflicts, social safety net, the pandemic, the divisive U.S. political situation, and inflation can be overwhelming. I remain committed, however, to the belief that engaged, motivated, and respected teams and people will perform at high levels.

As a consultant and advisor now, through my work at Archer Gray Co-Lab, I see a variety of leaders and industries. I always say to our team that Co-Lab is hired out of vision or out of pain. The reality is that when a company calls in outside resources, it either needs additional talent and resources to drive its vision, or it has a problem that needs to be fixed. In my time as an advisor, I have seen and worked with both situations. I respect the confidentiality of our clients, but I do want to share some recent insights from our engagements to close out this chapter of learnings.

We are currently working with a diverse set of clients in a variety of industries. At the core of our work in always quality and storytelling. What I consistently observe is that the company is driven by the vision and culture of the leader and their direct report team. When you have a leader with a clear vision and a team moving in the same direction, you observe amazing action and results. I can also confirm that when you see a team without a clear focus or purpose, whose members all seem to be working in silos and with varying goals and efforts, it creates a mess and missed opportunities. The pandemic and remote or hybrid work locations can either accelerate positive momentum or exacerbate hidden dysfunction, and as a leader, you have to course correct. I believe it is our responsibility as leaders at any level on a team to keep our teams focused and effective. It has never been more challenging to lead effectively, but when you commit to building cultures that support and enable high-performing teams and individual growth, it can be a wonderful and rewarding experience.

I have had the pleasure of working with some amazing leaders in the nonprofit sector through my volunteer positions. Dr. Eliza Byard at GLSEN, Jon Stettner at Make-A-Wish International, Sarah Kate Ellis at GLAAD, and Jarrett Barrios at American Red Cross Los Angeles are all exceptional leaders and wonderful examples of team building and culture building. They all served and serve with passion, purpose, and vision. Nonprofit leadership is a constant swirl of fundraising, team motivation, volunteer training and activation, and board management. I feel some of our best leaders in the USA can actually be found in these vital organizations.

As I end Learning #8 and reflect on the stories I shared, it does strike me again that I did not talk enough about LGBTQ+ leaders I worked with and learned from, which makes me realize why I am undertaking this effort to begin with. We need to elevate and celebrate their stories and impact. I do want to share some stories of leaders I have worked with in the nonprofit and university communities as I have learned and grown with them as well.

Dr. James Wimbush at Indiana University is the dynamic leader of the Diversity, Equity, and Inclusion Department and the former leader of the Graduate School at the Bloomington and Indianapolis campuses. James is a scholar, a leader, a driver, and incredibly charismatic. James lives his authenticity as a black, gay man in a long-term interracial marriage. He leads with intelligence, compassion, foresight, and hard work. His southern roots shine through in his communication style and manners, but underneath he has a steel spine and strong moral fiber I admire greatly. James welcomed me into the DEI community as a part-time executive-in-residence and allowed me the privilege of working on some incredible projects that raised the visibility and viability of our queer community. The most important skill I learned from Dr. Wimbush is PATIENCE. He showed me the pace of change in a university environment is not the same as the corporate world and taught me how to manage my expectations with grace. That is a very important skill in my toolkit now.

David Jacobs, the founding chairman of the Queer Philanthropy Circle and a lifelong Hoosier donor and advisor, is another exemplary role model for authentic leadership in our community. David endowed the world-renowned Jacobs School of Music at Indiana University to honor his parents and has donated time, talent, and treasure for years to the IU family and community. David has been a mentor since I joined the Indiana University Foundation Board, and what I learned from him is TENACITY and PERSISTENCE. David singlehandedly encouraged the university and the foundation to adopt diversity language and policies into all of their materials, by-laws, and governing principles. He refused to give up this cause, and saw it through to its completion. At times, I know he grew weary of repeating the same thing over and over as it sometimes felt like it was falling on deaf ears, but he never stopped communicating and educating. His wisdom and guidance and vision will positively impact our alma mater for years, and I am honored to step into a leadership role in the QPC to continue to elevate and support his message.

Through my work with the LGBTQ+ Culture Center, I had the pleasure of meeting Carrick Moon when he was a rising junior on the Bloomington campus. When I met Carrick, he had been out as a transgender man for almost a year. I was immediately struck by their wisdom, confidence, charisma, and openness to my questions. Carrick taught me about proper pronoun use, the importance of family support, and his desire to make an impact on the Bloomington campus for the queer and trans communities. We spoke about plans to start a Queer Student Union (QSU) on campus. This was prior to the pandemic, and I applauded this idea and committed my personal support and the support of the Queer Philanthropy Circle (QPC). A few months later, Carrick and his fellow founding members launched the QSU and were visible and vocal on day one. I was so impressed with their commitment and professionalism. They dealt with bullying, resistance, and outright hostility, but our community came together for them and they continuously grew through all of the adversity. Along with the LGBTQ+ Alumni Association, the QPC did whatever we could, but we also knew this initiative had to be student led and owned. Carrick was consistently impressive, and I found myself wondering where that strength came from and how I had missed that gene somehow when I was a student.

Spending time with Carrick and his peers constantly inspired me and made me want to do even more to support their work.

My final story about Carrick occurred during spring semester of his junior year, at the height of the pandemic, when he informed me he was running for IU Student Government President. I honestly should not have been surprised by now, but again, I found myself thinking how far the community had come since I was student and admiring his incredible strength. Carrick led with and lived his authentic story. He never shied away from his truth and never got hostile or defensive. At 20 years old, he was more mature, focused, and driven than many people I knew who were twice his age. Carrick lost that election, ironically, to an out gay, Black student. Yes, that is right. The top two vote getters for the head of Bloomington Student Government in 2021 were both from the queer community. I call that progress. I call that amazing. I thank them for showing me their world and teaching me and listening to me. Ultimately, Carrick's greatest leadership gift is that he left the QSU in strong leadership hands for the next class, and I am confident it will be a strong and vital student group for years to come. The Queer Student Union (QSU) will continue to bring the queer community together, open doors, and push the boundaries of what is possible for LGBTQ+ students at Indiana University. That gives me hope and strength.

I often am asked how I have built my career and what makes me successful. I also get asked questions about my methodology and my approach to new jobs or situations. It feels like this learning is a good place for me to share some of my secrets and insights that I wish I had learned earlier in my career. 1) Find a company and role you are truly passionate about, something that gets you up in the morning with eagerness and keeps you awake at night thinking of the possibilities. 2) Examine the marketplace and the competition for your idea, product, or service. Survey the environment for what is and is not working, and then take a serious inventory of how you can compete and differentiate in the marketplace. What makes you and your work different, special, or unique? How will you make your company and your community better with your contributions? 3) By now, you know I have been successful due to my ability to build teams and attract and grow talent. To me, there is no better success than shared success. 4) Be sure to learn from your mistakes, failures, and miscues. No one is perfect. Just try not to repeat them! 5) Keep a balance in your life between your personal needs and your professional aspirations. Remember that life is short and always prioritize your family and their needs. 6) Take care of yourself physically, mentally, emotionally, and spiritually. Please do not be afraid to ask for help or admit you do not know something. I think this is a formula that works for me and can work for many of you reading this book now.

I hope these stories and reflections fully illustrated Learning #8 for you. My lifelong commitment to building high-performing teams and supporting individual growth and performance have paid off for me in so many ways. Writing this learning has flooded me with amazing memories and gratitude for the teams I have worked with around the world. I hope you all feel as proud as I do.

9 | *Selfish* Is Not a Bad Word

I was raised in a family and a household where being called self-ish usually resulted in a time out or a seat in the corner to "think about" what you had just done. *Selfish* was defined for me as not sharing or putting one's needs in front of others or generally terrorizing my sister with a childhood prank. In the innocence of childhood, I accepted my parents' definition and worked hard not to be branded as selfish. Branding and my various names and nicknames are a very interesting area to discuss in context of this learning.

I was born James David, the son of James Fredric and grandson of Marvin James and James Joseph. Notice anything? My mother consciously chose a different middle name for me because she did not want me to be a "Junior." She wanted me to have my own identity. From day one, I was called Jimmy. I also had an uncle named James and a cousin named James, all of who went by different nicknames. By the time I was born, Jimmy was the moniker that was left, and to this day, I am still Jimmy to my sister and most of my cousins. My Dad's nickname for me was James Davido . . . and I was only called James or James David when I was being selfish or otherwise in trouble.

Now as a branding and marketing advisor, it strikes me that these various nicknames actually represented and continue to repre-sent different parts of my personality. Jimmy is playful, laughs a lot, hates to be tickled, and is still innocent of many of the ways the world works. He also is incredibly selfish. James David is the troublemaker, the shit stirrer, the smart mouth, and the most likely to be on some form of grounding or time out. Jim is the name I used when I started school, is my "work" name, and the name I am most called. It was also my Dad's name brand, so it created issues as I grew and we became Big Jim and Little Jim or Old Jim and Young Jim, neither names my Dad liked very much. It especially became an issue when I got to the same size as my Dad and you could hear confused callers to our one line house phone when someone did not know we had the same name.

Jim is the worrier, the caretaker, the responsible one, and the one with stress. Jim attends therapy and reads a lot of self-help books. Jim is also an introverted extrovert, which confuses a lot of people in his life. You see, I need my alone and private time, and I love being alone with my thoughts and to do selfish things now. It recharges my batteries and allows me to be more extroverted and social and giving most of the time.

What I have learned, with the benefit of smart therapists, coaches, and the wisdom of time is that being selfish is actually practicing self-care. I am so grateful I finally figured that out and I hope that by sharing this learning with you, you can figure it out earlier in your life and benefit from my path. Feeding your soul and taking private time for reflection, rest, and restoration is not wrong; it is essential. I also have learned the important but subtle differences among caring, care taking, care giving, and controlling. I know many friends and relatives are laughing at that sentence because I can easily slip into anal, control-freak mode. I can take caring to an overreactive and almost scary place. Practice, not perfection! At least I recognize and own that part of me now. I have worked hard to live with more spontaneity and surprise in my life. I have learned to let other people plan and own activities. In fact, I pull back now from volunteering to be a planner or organizer.

Later in life, my Mom started called me J.D. I do not remember where or when it began, but I kind of like it. Maybe because I like J.D. Salinger? Most likely, it is because it felt like something that was uniquely mine, my brand. A name that honored my Dad and my family and the history of James in our legacy, but allowed me to explore the world with my own calling card and uniqueness. To be honest, I used J.D. for my online dating profiles too. I think it felt incognito and confidential and safe. No one could google J.D. Fielding and find much information about me, if anything.

Here is what I like about J.D. He is a true combination of all the aspects of ME. One of my favorite quotes is Picasso's about all children being artists, and how we just need to remember that when we become adults. I crave that feeling of freedom, whimsy, and innocence that Jimmy had. I was never a totally carefree child, often called too smart for my own good, but I did once know how to run, skip, sing with abandon, and play hide and seek. I loved art class with Ms. Archambeau and even got to attend a Saturday workshop at the Toledo Museum of Art for young artists. We used to come home from school and change into our "play clothes" and run outside to find our friends. We would do random and silly kid things until we heard our Mom's whistle or bell or until the streetlights came on . . . whichever came first. I remember the simple joys of catching fireflies in a jar, Halloween adventures, and the smell of freshly cut summertime lawns. Kickball, dodgeball, softball, ring around the rosey were so much FUN! As I mentioned earlier, I grew up pretty fast and was probably "old" before my time, but I do fondly remember those days, the magic of jumping in piles of leaves; making snow angels, igloos, and snowball fights; cannonballs into the pool. Jimmy is in J.D. for sure.

James David is in there, too. The disciplined, ambitious, and smart overachiever, who is constantly striving for approval and public validation. James gets tired and needs the recharge time. James can be obnoxious. James can be tiresome. People like him though because he gets things done and he is predictable and dependable. He is described as steady. It has taken me a lifetime to fully appreciate and love all aspects of my personality unconditionally. Determining how to integrate these pieces of me has been a lifelong experiment and it is constantly evolving. As I age and experience more, as the world changes, as my family changes, I need to update the best and worst parts of me.

Part of my authentic leadership journey is embracing all of me, but also setting boundaries with what parts of me I use or show in professional settings. Being authentic does not equal oversharing. You have to read and know your audience and your team members, and only share what works for the group and what you are comfortable with sharing. I am not saying be inauthentic or hide your truth, but I am advocating for sensitivity and decorum. Remember, living your truth is also educational and serves as a role model for your team, and also allows the team to work and be fully present authentically. I strive to never impose my thinking or opinion on anyone, but I will never hide who I truly am anymore. LinkedIn is a perfect illustration for this narrative. I view and use that platform as my professional social media community and enjoy the updates and posts from my network. I do not use it, however, to share updates about my personal life. I see a very clear boundary there. I am always authentically me and post what is important to me, but I do believe in that separation. My personal updates, when I am so moved, can be found on Instagram, where I have a much tighter and vetted community for that type of content and storytelling. Again, I do not see this as being inauthentic, I think it is being respectful and establishing boundaries. It is a very important distinction and insight.

One of my more recent learnings about self-care as I enter my late 50s is a concept I have coined "20 More Summers." No matter how hard you try, how much you work out, and how well you eat, your body and mind age. I firmly believe we have to do everything we can to age gracefully and without drama, but the march of time is inevitable and unavoidable. I always say I just want to stay vital. I am not being morbid or pessimistic, just realistic. My father and both my grandfathers passed away at 72 or younger. My grandmothers made it to 96 and 101, and my Mom is a relatively physically healthy 81-year-old albeit with early stages of dementia. I am conscious of the years passing quickly and the male mortality statistics. The concept of 20 More Summers has to do with my annual seasonal relocation to the Leelanau Peninsula in Michigan and the shores of Lake Michigan. My summers there are a wonderful escape, an excuse to connect with old friends and family, connect to nature, and connect to my childhood.

It was during one of those trips, as I was enjoying a glass of wine with friends one pink sunset evening, that it hit me. I was then in my early 50s, and given my family history, realized I may only have 20 more summers in my lifetime. Acknowledging that possibility became a type of rallying cry for me and my closest friends. For example, I encouraged dear friends to accelerate buying a lake house, urging them not to wait for better times or rates, but saying, "Remember, 20 more summers!" Traveling to Europe, even at the height of crowded tourist season and a pandemic is due to this mentality. Basically, time is precious, life is short, and the question to ask yourself is: How are you going to use this gift of time? To me, it is the ultimate selfish or self-care filter. If you had a crystal ball and could see your future, how would you use your time, especially in the glorious summer season? For me, the sunshine, the freshwater, the trees, and the clean air of Up North is high on that list. Time with friends and family is critical as well. I hear a clock and see a calendar in my head, but it is not ominous or scary . . . it is just a great reminder to take care of myself and my needs. Never take anything for granted. Live fully and authentically and use your precious commodity of time wisely.

All of us deal with the aging of our parents and this process is very challenging for all involved. I have watched my friends with admiration as they navigated their family's needs. It is another obvious selfish learning and highlights the need for self-care and balancing that with caretaking requirements for those you love.

My sister and I recently made a difficult decision that many of my peers face at this stage in our lives. Over the last two summers, our mother has suffered a serious fall, endured two major surgeries, and been diagnosed with early stage dementia. Mom moved to a 55+ community in 2015, three years after our Dad's passing. She sold the home they shared and found herself a place she loved, for the first time completely on her own. She was very proud of her home, made a lot of good friends, and was content. The dementia, however, had other plans for her. We went through a "Silver Alert" when she got lost in her car with her dog one day and her cell phone lost service and battery. After her fall, she was airlifted from northern Arizona to a trauma center. She began to miss bill payments, double pay other bills, and throw away important paperwork. It is, sadly, a common story. My sister was the primary contact and caregiver due to location, and I took over all of Mom's banking and finances.

After another surgery and recovery in the summer of 2022, in consultation with her excellent doctor, we decided to move Mom to an independent/assisted living home. I conducted the search, and over three days, visited eight different facilities, a tour I dubbed "the good, the bad, and the ugly." It was sobering to see what Mom's future could look like. We are grateful that Mom and Dad were insured, which gave us some very important options. Look at your long-term care insurance options = BIG HINT!

Moving Mom into her new apartment, going through her belongings, making donations, and throwing away memories was surprisingly emotional for me. It dredged up a lifetime of stories, happy memories, and pain. We found family documents and photos I had never seen in my life. I found the typed-out eulogy from my Dad's memorial service that knocked the wind out of my chest. I felt the roles change again as my sister and I became the decision makers and the caregivers as our Mom's dependence on us grows by the day. She is losing her short-term memory. She can no longer drive as she gets confused and has lost executive function.

My sister and I were losing sleep with constant nervous energy and scenario planning. I know everyone goes through this at some point, and I know we will age and need assistance. I just wanted Mom to do it gracefully, and it feels and felt very abrupt. I just kept hearing my Dad's last words to me: "Take care of your Mom, you know she cannot do it herself." Of course, I would take care of my Mom, I had been doing it my whole life, but the gravitas of his words constantly echo in my head. I realize this process has been a culmination of so many life experiences and learnings, many of which I have shared in this book. I have leaned on my sister and my friends and read anything I can find about her disease and this transition process. Dealing with Mom's transition put me in the self-care mode too. I double-checked my long-term care insurance policy, looked at my will, trust, and advanced care directive, and talked to my sister and my partner about my plans. Again, it is not selfish to acknowledge your needs and wants. I want to rely on myself and my resources to ensure I have the best care and services available when I need them, especially when I am at my most vulnerable.

It is shocking how draining and emotional this process with my Mom has been for all of us. I called my dearest friends and told them I wanted to make deposits together on a wonderful five-star long-term care facility so we could grow old together and around familiar faces. My theory is that when I cannot remember certain things in my past, my friends will fill in the gaps. I also feel safe to be around people who love me unconditionally as I age. If they have already seen me at my best and my worst in our youth and those scary college stories, they should be able to handle the aging process with me. In moments of clarity in my 90s, I want to see these friends and smile.

It is an odd truth for most of the queers in my generation. We do not have children who will be part of our care decisions or options. I also realized during the search for my Mom about the lack of viable senior living options for the queer community. In one beautiful center in Scottsdale, Arizona, I even suggested a Pride Wing to the sales office as a legitimate need and marketing opportunity. It is a concerning gap in the market that I plan to do more research on in the coming years.

In the area of self-care, I recently have uncovered two interesting opportunities based on advancements in science. They are both making me think deeply and presenting some interesting discussions and decisions. For the fact-based control-freak side of me, they are especially challenging.

The first opportunity is in the area of genetic testing and the mapping of the human genome. I have been watching the developments in this area with interest, especially in the work St Jude's is doing on mapping the genomes for children's cancer. At my recent executive physical, I learned of the advancements in identifying the marker for pancreatic cancer, my father's cause of death. I met with a genetic ethicist and counselor and learned of the amazing research and updates. It is now possible to examine my markers and indicators for pancreatic cancer in a way that is very similar to the work in breast cancer mapping. I listened, learned, and took the information home to discuss with my sister and my partner. To date, I have not made a final decision on how or if to proceed. Type A me wants to know. The softer, gentler J.D. is skeptical because there is nothing to do or to be gained with the knowledge. I have several female friends who have had therapeutic mastectomies based on their test results and family history. I applaud their strength and active ownership of their bodies and self-care. I think that is what I am struggling with in my decision. It is the ultimate "So, what?" test. If I know I have the marker or indicator, how will that impact me? It is better to know or not know? Would I drastically change my life if I had new facts?

Another recent discovery occured when I did ancestry DNA testing as part of a genealogy push I felt when my Dad passed away. There was validation for many things I had been told about my genetic background, but one new insight really stuck out. We (me and my sister) are in the 1% club globally for Neanderthal DNA. Basically, we have really old DNA and can be genetically traced back for many generations. To be clear, the Neanderthal period was between 40,000 and 100,000 years ago. Combined with our Nordic, Northern European, and British Isles DNA, we have been roaming the earth for a long time!

This knowledge has become an interesting hobby for me and Jill. We read anything we can get our hands on and go down internet rabbit holes. One interesting current learning is that our DNA may provide some Covid-19 resistance, and neither one of us has been infected to date. We are consistently contacted by the DNA testing firm to participate in studies. Science is fascinating and scary! It is just another source of information I can use in my self-care routine and regimen. And it is kind of great for cocktail party chatter! It also makes me understand why sometimes I feel like I have been carrying burdens for a very long time and have lived many lives before this one. Now, I have factual DNA data that supports my reality and intuition.

My final piece of advice in this area is what I have learned about envy and jealousy and the negative impacts they have on your self-esteem and self-care focus. I think social media can be a big source of these feelings and doubts, even though I understand and embrace its use and needs. I find myself, at times, surfing through LinkedIn and reading new job information and director roles for my peers and network. It is hard to admit, but I can get really jealous and go down some dangerous rabbit holes with this exercise. I find myself wondering why I did not know about this opportunity or why wasn't I contacted? My mind can race with various scenarios and answers, and it is simply unhealthy. It triggers my lifelong insecurities and I find it frustrating and almost embarrassing that I cannot always control it well. I am proud of my career, my current role, my charity work, and my work history. Yet, there are times I cannot keep myself from comparing myself to others.

Please learn early on in your life and career to not compare yourself to others. Set goals for yourself, find a mentor, measure progress, and find joy and satisfaction in personal growth and new learnings. True success is not measured by title or compensation or promotions. I know . . . easy for me to say, but I swear it is true. If I could do it over again, I would have stopped along the way in my career to smell the roses as my Mom always used to ask me to do.

I often find myself wondering if there is a glass ceiling for queer people. I am excited to see the advancement of initiatives to diversify boardrooms and evolve from the cisgender white patriarchy that has dominated the business world. I am grateful for states like California that are mandating gender diversity and representation on boards and in the C-suite, but I do not know if it is enough. Systemic change moves at a snail's pace. I am not sure if it was my arrogance or my naïveté that had me assuming I would be on more boards of directors by now. I have an interesting and diverse background, a history of leadership roles, and a plethora of experience in C-suites and on charitable boards, but it does not seem to be enough to get me into consideration. I am offered plenty of start-up advisory roles and sweat equity positions, but to date have not seen director opportunities. Ironically, when I was at Disney, I had many board role calls, but we were not allowed to serve on for-profit boards. Then, as a sitting CEO at Claire's, I had numerous options, but I chose to pass and focus on my company's needs and business. I talked about not living with regrets, but in this area, I do have a few. It has been a good lesson for me, and I will continue to learn and grow and trust that this is all part of a grand plan. I just have to learn how to control that little green nuisance called envy.

When I first began consulting, I would take any job or project that came along as I was so worried about missing out on something

and constantly worrying about how I would find other opportunities. It triggered both my FOMO insecurities and my envy
issues, which is not a pleasant combination. You really have to
work on your self-talk to avoid going down these rabbit holes
and falling into pits of jealousy. It is not productive at all. A commitment to self-care is a personal daily struggle for me, and I am
consistently working on developing new habits and techniques
to stay on track. Keep yourself in balance and maintain realistic
goals. You will be happier and more productive with this focus.
Let them call you SELFISH and wear it with pride.

10 | Authentic Kindness Is More Important than Being Right or First

I try to live my life in a state of constant gratitude. It is not always easy, and sometimes I slip into pity party mode, but I can usually snap myself out of it quickly. My final learning is about moving through life as a compassionate leader is the simple joy of being kind and supportive to yourself and others. It should be easy to do for everyone, but I have learned it is not always the case. Do not be hard on yourself. No one is perfect. You will be rewarded for your efforts, even if it is not about immediate feedback and gratification. Being queer does not automatically make you kind, and I know plenty of mean-spirited people of all genders and gender identities. Believe me, I can be harsh and impatient and quick to temper, but I do try to move through life with a smile and a kind word for everyone. It is also true that I am competitive and I like to challenge myself and my teams. As I have matured, though, I realized how you achieve goals is as important, if not more important, than the actual result. Kindness does not equal weakness or passiveness; one should still be passionate and commit to fighting for what is right. My guidance is, however, to do it in a compassionate and caring way. I will always fight for and support what I believe is right, but I will aways lead with kindness.

I do believe that being insecure and seeking approval and validation as a kid made me overly sensitive to the needs and feelings of others. Recently, at my high school reunion, I was approached by one of my elementary school classmates, someone I was at Meadowvale with from kindergarten through the 7th grade. It was great to see him and catch up. He caught me off guard when he asked for a private moment and chat. He thanked me. I asked, for what? He then proceeded to tell me a story about 4th and 5th grade when our desks were next to each other. We used to do a lot of reading aloud assignments in those classes, especially in social studies and English sections. He thanked me for helping him quietly under my breath and giving him words he did not know when it was his turn to read aloud. To be honest, I did not remember doing this. He did, however, and said I helped through two solid school years and never once made him feel less than other students or inferior. He admitted to me he had a slight learning disability and a tremendous fear of these assignments, but he came to rely on me and my friendship to get him through.

I was shocked. I had no idea that he had struggled with this, or that I helped him without thinking. Remember, this was in the 1970s. People did not talk about learning challenges. Classes were big, and teachers were very good, but they did not have time to slow down an entire class to help individual students. This friend and I talked for over 30 minutes and I left that conversation with so much respect for him and with so much gratitude for his sharing. His honesty and vulnerability were touching and authentic. Simple, random acts of kindness and compassion have lifelong lasting impacts, and I am grateful he shared that memory and reminded me of that fact.

The process of aging is inevitable and can be quite daunting. The physical changes are real, and at times, I look in the mirror and see my Dad looking back at me! Yes, with age comes wisdom, and I appreciate my hard-earned wisdom. I enjoy my lifetime of stories and memories, and the things I have learned through trial and error. I have always been very good at juggling multiple priorities and keeping lots of balls in the air, but I have had to learn what truly to prioritize. At this point in my life and career, I am very careful to choose whom I work with and the kinds of projects on which to focus my energy. I realize that not everyone has that luxury, but I do encourage people to carefully consider how and where to spend their energy. It is a precious commodity.

★ ★ ★

During the pandemic, I had many opportunities for self-reflection, especially in the California lock-down period. I found some amazing tools and resources that I want to share.

First, the power of journaling. I have always been a journal keeper, but I found myself returning to it like an old friend during those solitary days. The practice allows me to capture memories on paper and to let go of some baggage simultaneously. There is no right way or technique to journal . . . for me, I need an inspirational notebook and a great pen that feels good in my hand. I need to commit to it daily at first to re-engage the muscle memory, but after that, I can do it intermittently and it serves the same purpose.

Another new practice learned in this period is the act of mindfulness and meditation. The advances in technology really enabled this new skill, with apps like Calm and Ten Percent Happier leading the way. I also read Dan Harris's book *10% Happier* and loved his simple and authentic storytelling; it really sparked my own path to mindfulness. Through Coursera, I attended the Science of Well-Being course taught by Yale professor Dr. Laurie Santos. That was an amazing course, and I learned so many new facts. It blew my mind to learn about the scientific foundation of happiness and that you could truly learn to be happy with exercise and attention. When I posted about my experience with this course on LinkedIn, I was not totally surprised to find others in my network who had taken the course as well. That experience was one of the many unexpected gifts and benefits of the pandemic.

I've also done a lot of reading in the last few years, and found two topic areas very helpful. One was revisiting my overseas study experience in Denmark, and studying why the Danes are consistently ranked as the happiest people in the world. It reminded me why I was so truly happy and engaged almost 40 years ago, and I committed to spending more time on a regular basis in

Denmark. I am also very excited that my niece, Samantha, is planning her junior year abroad in Copenhagen. To watch her experience that culture will be a gift and a joy. It also gives me a great excuse to re-engage in that amazing culture.

I also have recently discovered and embraced the Japanese concept of *ikigai*, meaning "a reason for being," or I have also seen it described as "life in balance." Ikigai is the intersection of four circles: your passion, mission, vocation, and profession. More simply put: it is the intersection of what you LOVE, what the world NEEDS, what you are GOOD AT, and what you can be PAID FOR. Simple, yet elegant and so important as a life guide tool.

Studying both the Danish culture and this ikigai concept made me realize the intense connections between these countries and the energy I feel whenever I visit them. Japan is one of my favorite countries in the world: the culture, the fashion, the architecture, the cuisine, the respect for elders and family, and the vitality of longevity are wonderful. A recent visit to Denmark with my Mom and niece evoked those same kind of feelings. Copenhagen feels like a city with a soul, conscience, and vital heartbeat. The energy is palpable, and there is a tangible feeling everywhere that anything is possible. People of all ages seem to have a vibrancy and zest for life that is infectious. I also love their societal commitment to alternative energy, sustainable communities, and controlling climate change aggressively. Thinking about my time as a student there, I realize that I was very happy and more relaxed there than any other time in college. I should have paid more attention to that fact. Why am I sharing all of this? It is simple . . . I really hope we can find more kindness and simple happiness in the world.

One of my other overused phrases is "Keep Smiling." I have used it as a sign-off on my emails for years and I love to see people smile. There is something so open and kind and wonderful about an authentic smiling face. It is just so much easier to focus on positive energy and outcomes. I am not advocating being unrealistic or unnaturally cheery, just more optimistic than pessimistic when possible.

I am also a great believer in moving through life with a healthy dose of humility and self-awareness. I always say how much I admire confidence and abhor arrogance. Navigating Hollywood for over 20 years has taught me the difference on many occasions. After years of insecurity and awkwardness, I can feel myself moving with more grace and purpose, and I hope, confidence. I know who I am, what I stand for, what my boundaries are, what my needs are, and I hope I am a better friend and more empathetic leader because of it.

An excellent example of kindness in action is the 2022 passing of the Respect for Marriage Act. To be honest, I never expected to see gay and interracial marriage codified into law in my lifetime. I watched with surprise and happiness as a bilateral group of senators and representatives actually listened to their constituents and their communities, and voted with their head and their heart. It is a wonderful example of keeping an open mind and leading with kindness. I wish we could use the same sentiments to address gun ownership laws.

I love the concepts of random acts of kindness, paying it forward, and doing good deeds for others. I believe the world needs more emphasis on what are often called softer skills and sometimes are not as valued as hard/technical skills. I value EQ as much as I value IQ. I hope we can elevate and celebrate civility, kindness, gratitude, and simply helping others again in our communities. We are in control of our actions, our attitudes, and our reactions. Leading authentically with pride, controlling our egos, and keeping our priorities in order can lead to so many unexpected wonders. Remember, life is a journey, and a great sweeping story of adventure, love, grief, pain, and joy. Build communities of support and guidance.

My amazing Grandma Fielding lived 101 years with a smile on her face every day of her journey, including as she passed peacefully in her sleep. She always told me to think of life as a roller coaster ride or a merry-go-round. The merry-go-round was safe, predictable, and moved at an easy cadence. Roller coasters have slow and fast moments, dips, thrills, and steep drops. They feel more unpredictable and almost out of control. Grandma encouraged me to choose more roller coasters. I hope you do the same. I honor her wisdom and life by trying to follow her example.

I will not lie, it is not always easy to lead with kindness, and at times, I can get very hot and passionate about perceived wrongs and injustices. I am tested often, and I learn from all of these challenges. Currently, I am struggling with many politicians and civic leaders who seem to be attacking core principles and learnings in the name of pushing back against so-called "woke" culture. Their removing books from classrooms and libraries, removing AP courses that teach Black history, and attacking families of trans children who seek safe and gender-affirming medical care enrage me and scare me. In my current home state of Georgia, there is legislation pending that would outlaw and criminalize any conversations with children about sexuality or gender identity. Think about what these legislators are doing. Cutting off compassionate care and fact-based discussions with all children, but especially vulnerable children who may be questioning their identity, could have devastating and far-reaching impacts for years. As I said earlier, just by living my authentic life, I have become an activist. I wish I could make it easier for all of us to just get along and stay focused on our own lives, but I do not see a choice. I have to speak out; I have to say something when things are just not right. I do not like to confront anyone or argue often, but I have a mission to educate and inform and speak my truth.

I am ending this learning and this book with the ultimate act of kindness. I am going to forgive myself. I am going to love and accept myself unconditionally. This project has brought back so many emotions, both amazing and terrifying, and I realize I have to fully forgive myself and let go to fully embrace the rest of my life. To be fully present and open to the new possibilities of the world, I need to not live or dwell in the past. I purposely chose a picture of five-year-old Jimmy for my Zoom photo placeholder. I am dressed in my red and black holiday suit and I am sitting on my grandparents' sofa. I have an amazing and natural smile on my face. I am not riddled with insecurities and self-doubt. I do not know I am gay yet, although I do think I asked for an Easy-Bake oven that holiday (I know—stereotype!). That Jimmy is innocent, imaginative, playful, and curious. My inner saboteur and negative self-talk have not kicked in to gear yet. That Jimmy is not worried about his weight, his hair loss, his aching knees, or his career. He does not care about a legacy or what other people really think about him. He does not need or seek external validation. He values his family and friends and tries to slow down and live in the moment.

Be kind to yourself; be kind to others; be kind to the earth. Life is not a race to riches or glory. The key is to determine early what your authentic path looks like and to have the courage to go on that journey. At one point in my life, as an out gay man, I realized I had a choice to be invisible or invincible. It was not an easy path, but I used my strength to push forward, and I hope others can do the same. As I said earlier, just by living your authentic life openly and proudly, you are an activist and educator. So many people in the United States and around the world cannot live openly as it is too dangerous or life threatening, so we must help them by elevating and celebrating our own stories loudly and proudly.

As much as I hope you and other readers have found some guidance and wisdom in my stories, I now realize that doing this book was an incredibly selfish act. So, I am going to be kind to myself and give myself some freedom from past mistakes and regrets. Stay proud; stay humble; cherish your family and friends; love with abandon; and dance and sing with joy. Work on projects you love and that make a positive difference in your community.

Jimmy, you done good! You are right where you are supposed to be and you are not done yet. Please remember also to help others live safe, productive, and authentic lives. You have a responsibility to give back and pay it forward. The Community needs you to be your best and most authentic self. Do not waste any more time on seeking external validation or quick fixes; just live every day with simple gratitude and joy. Love yourself and let's take care of each other.

Epilogue

"We are all in the gutter, but some of us are looking at the stars."

— Oscar Wilde

I love this quote on so many levels. First, I love Oscar Wilde's intelligence, artistry, and talent. His stories have brought me endless hours of joy and transported me to some amazing places. Our community owes a lot to Mr. Wilde's tenacity and the trials, the bigotry, and harassment he faced for living authentically and simply loving another man.

This quote also speaks to the eternal optimist in me, as writing this book has made me realize there is still so much I want to do with my life and time. It also keeps me grounded and humble. I never want to start a day without practicing gratitude. I really am trying to stop and smell the roses as my Mom always advised.

Thank you for taking this journey of reflection with me. I hope you learned something along the way, and you are able to take something interesting and informative with you from your effort. It has taken me over 50 years to feel what I feel today . . .

happy. I hope you get there faster than I did, and that you enjoy the trip. Happiness is possible and finding your community and authentic path is magical.

I always say I keep moving forward and that I do not live with regrets, but I am lying to myself. I have so many regrets and things I wish I could do over. Most of them are because I did not have the strength or the courage to embrace myself completely at a younger age. I am so hopeful for this current generation. I do, however, want to apologize to this current generation and especially my nieces, my godchildren, and the children of my dearest friends. Some days I watch the news and just shake my head in disbelief. Climate change, war, sociopolitical tension, and the Supreme Court both scare and frustrate me. The latest horror is the random banning of books and editing of student newspapers for content called queer or gay, or content which illuminates our racist history in the United States.

Judgmental and ill-informed adults are making horrible and far-reaching decisions for children who deserve to be fully educated. We just need to get out of the way and stop building obstacles for them. It is time for 80-year-old CEOs, regardless of experience and skill, to gracefully step aside and allow new ideas and leadership into the positions of power and decision-making authority. Watch what is happening in Congress as an example of moving on with grace and wisdom. Writing this book has made me realize how much work there is left on my personal journey and to help make a difference in the world. Like the country and society overall, I am a work in progress. It feels nice to not feel finished. . . . I hope I can add value and make a difference for many more years. Feel free to stay in touch with me at my website and follow me on social media. Our connection and community make me and all of us stronger:

www.allpridenoego.com

In addition, if you want to learn more about how to help people find and support their authentic selves, consider volunteering or donating to one of the following amazing nonprofit organizations.

Resource list

GLSEN (www.glsen.org)

Trevor Project (www.thetrevorproject.org)

GLAAD (www.glaad.org)

Human Rights Campaign (www.hrc.org)

Indiana University Foundation (www.iufoundation.iu.edu)

Indiana University Department of Diversity, Equity, and Inclusion (www.diversity.iu.edu)

National Center for Transgender Equality (www.transequality .org)

Southern Christian Leadership Conference (www.nationalsclc .org)

Planned Parenthood (www.plannedparenthood.org)

It Gets Better Project (www.itgetsbetter.org)

Indiana University Queer Student Union (Instagram @qsuiu)

Acknowledgments

There are so many people to thank and recognize for their incredible support of this project. Like most things in life, it takes a village of wise people, supporters, and challengers to complete a book project. I am grateful to you all, especially my early readers and feedback crew.

First, I have to recognize my families (birth, chosen, and work). All of you contributed to this book with your patience, encouragement, and belief.

The 4 Js—Janice, Jill, James F., and James D. (me!). You have been on this journey with me for almost 60 years, and I cannot believe how blessed I am to call you Mom, Sister, and Dad. I miss you, Dad, every day of my life and I feel your strength and support from above. I hope this makes you proud.

My chosen family, my lifelong friends, . . . you know what you mean to me, and I hope you feel your impact in these words and stories. You have been there for me through all of the ups and downs, and literally lifted me up physically and emotionally when I was at my lowest points. Now, you have given me access to your incredible children and their families, and I cherish my time with them. I love this next chapter of our lives we are opening and I cannot wait to see where we go and to spend precious time together.

To my queer posse, the amazing LGBTQ+ people in my life, thank you for loving me unconditionally and for making me dance with joy and abandon. I learned how to be proud from you. I learned how to love myself from you. I learned how to be an activist from you and when and how to call out injustices. I learned how to celebrate and live out loud from you as well. Your support enables me to flourish.

My work families and the teams I have had the privilege of working with and working for over the years, I thank you for letting me make mistakes, and grow, and for trying new things with me. I am grateful for the memories and the education.

I want to thank my current work teams and partners at Archer Gray for continuing my development and education and allowing me the space and time to complete this project. I am very proud to work with all of you.

I thank the amazing Amanda Miller for over 40 years of friendship and the courage to chase my dreams. From our conversations in Toledo to our New York City theater and dinner evenings, you have been a constant and grounding force in my life.

To the Wiley Team, especially Shannon Vargo, Jeanenne Ray, Michelle Hacker, Sangeetha Suresh, and Jozette Moses . . . thank you for taking the chance on a first-time author and sharing my vision for this book. Your support has been wonderful.

I owe Julie Kerr, my amazing editor, a huge debt of gratitude for shepherding me through the process and for her direct and honest feedback and her tolerance for a first-time author.

To the queer trailblazers and role models who came before me, I thank you for your efforts to create change in society so I had the ability to live my authentic life and have such a wonderful career. I stand on the foundation you laid.

To my bosses, mentors, guides, coaches, and therapists . . . thank you for listening without judgment and challenging me to accept my truths. I grew because of all of you. I know I could be challenging to manage at times, but your efforts are appreciated and I hope I am paying your teachings forward every day.

To my mentees, my trainees, and the young people in my life—I thank you for giving me so much hope for the future of our community and planet. Katie and Sammie, you know that being your "guncle" is an absolute joy and the best role in my life. To my godchildren, Sara, Roman, and Lola, it is a privilege to support you and watch you blossom and make your mark on the world. To all of the under-30 readers out there, thank you for scaring me (in a good way) and showing me true innovation and new viewpoints and perspectives. I cannot wait to live in the world you create.

Finally, to JJWL, dear Joseph. Thank you for your passionate commitment to living a positive, impactful life and for showing me that unconditional love was possible, even in my 50s. Your intelligence, compassion, and ambition inspire me and keep me young and energized. I love the life we are building and how you challenge me to keep growing and learning. Your encyclopedic knowledge of music and your infectious dance energy bring life to our home and every venue you enter. Your family's embrace of me and us is amazing and nurturing as well. We are very blessed. You make every day special.

About the Author

An experienced and respected retail and media industry veteran, Jim Fielding has built his successful career and expertise at the intersection of quality storytelling, innovative product and merchandising, and compelling consumer experiences.

Jim currently serves as a partner at Archer Gray, an independent media company, focusing his energies on building businesses, products, and experiences for its ecosystem of creators and client partners. He also proudly served as a part-time Executive-in-Residence for IU Ventures and The Office of Diversity, Equity, and Inclusion at Indiana University.

Jim spent the bulk of his career leading consumer products groups at the world's largest media companies, including Disney, Dreamworks, Awesomeness TV, and Twentieth Century Fox. A known culture and team builder, he has built diverse and visionary teams that have excelled in challenging and competitive marketplaces globally. Jim spent four years as president of Disney Stores Worldwide, completely redefining the digital and physical experience around the globe. He also served as CEO of Claire's Stores, Inc., the world's leading destination for teen jewelry and accessories.

Jim's early experience was firmly rooted in leading global retail companies, including stints at Dayton Hudson, The Gap, Lands' End, and J. Peterman Company. He built an extensive knowledge base in all aspects of vertical specialty retail, including supply chain, product design, store operations, and visual merchandising.

An active community leader and philanthropist, Jim currently serves on the board of directors for the Indiana University Foundation and was a founding member of the Dean's Council for the Hamilton Lugar Global and International School. Jim is a founder of the Queer Philanthropy Circle, a first-in-the-country fundraising and advocacy group for the queer community. Jim also participates in the Women's Philanthropic Leadership Circle and the Black Philanthropy Circle. In addition, Jim is a former board member for GLSEN, Make-A-Wish International, and American Red Cross. He has endowed a number of scholarships at Indiana University to support overseas study experiences, international internships, and advocacy leadership training.

Jim currently lives in Atlanta, Georgia, with his partner, Joseph, and their dogs, Cricket and Olive. In the summers, you will find them in Leland and Northport, Michigan.

Index